WARNE'S TRANSPORT LIBRARY

Farm Tractors

Compiled by Nick Baldwin

FREDERICK WARNE, London and New York

ACKNOWLEDGEMENTS

To compile the list of current world-wide tractor manufacturers, every known firm was contacted during the winter of 1976/77. All those which had supplied adequate information by 31st March 1977 were included. Many manufacturers went out of their way to be helpful and the author would particularly like to thank Hannu Niskanen of Valmet (Finland), David Heisler and the late Frank Hollis of International Harvester (Great Britain), John Briscoe of Massey-Ferguson, E. L. Briggs of Muir Hill and Martin Hayes of British Leyland.

In the historic section the author is indebted to the publishers of the recent *Old Motor Kaleidoscope of 1895–1955 Farm Tractors*, 17 Air Street, London W1, for permission to use several of the photographs from the *Old Motor* archives. Other photographs came from the author's collection, from the Museum of English Rural Life at Reading University, where John Creasey was most helpful, and from several of the pioneer manufacturers that are still producing tractors. The excellent view of the 1902 Ivel is by courtesy of the National Motor Museum, Beaulieu, Hants.

Finally, grateful thanks to Charles Cawood in Yorkshire and to Robert Crawford in Lincolnshire, who were endless sources of useful advice and photographs.

ISBN 0 7232 2060 3

Filmset and printed in Great Britain by
BAS Printers Limited, Over Wallop, Hampshire
2618·777

For every ten words written about the history, development or current state of the motor-car, hardly a word has appeared in print about the farm tractor. Yet the tractor has played just as large a part in world mechanization, and indeed can be claimed to have been of far more direct benefit to mankind than practically all other motor-driven machines.

In this book the significant steps taken by tractor designers since the internal combustion engine appeared some ninety years ago have been examined. The early motor replacement for the horse was followed by the crawler, the first frameless tractor in 1912, the beginnings of mass production in the First World War, the implement lift and power take off that revolutionized implement design, the diesel engine, the pneumatic tyre, and all the other significant events which have contributed to the sophisticated tractors of today.

Moving on to current production, details are given of the background to over seventy world-wide manufacturers, and examples from their range are studied. The handful of giant multi-national companies naturally receive the greatest coverage because of their lion's share of the market. However, dozens of smaller firms are examined as well to show their often ingenious solution to specialized agricultural problems. Among these firms are some specializing in giant machines, able to cover hundreds of acres per day, special tractors on stilts for working above row crops, miniature or specially narrow tractors for working between rows of vines, and low centre of gravity, all-wheel drive tractors for mountain farmers. There are simple types of machine that are being produced in the newly-developing countries— tractors which have often reverted to separate chassis for easier and cheaper production.

The subject is so vast that it has been necessary to limit attention to true agricultural tractors, and miniature garden and horticultural tractors of under 20 bhp have thus been excluded. Likewise self-propelled machines intended for only one or two agricultural purposes are not represented, but may one day be the subject of a companion to this volume.

It has been a fascinating task unearthing the information to be found in the following pages, and it is hoped that not only farmers, but transport enthusiasts of all types will find it equally intriguing.

Nick Baldwin

1907

1917

1939

1947

1952

1955

1968

1970s

Fords over the years demonstrate the evolution of the tractor.

The invention of the internal combustion engine in the 1880s brought mechanization to agriculture, just as it did to road transport. Before that, the draught animal and human power had reigned supreme, apart from the efforts of the steam pioneers from about 1850 onwards. The early steam-engines were well suited to power stationary machinery, but when they came to draw implements their enormous weight caused damage to the land and frequent bogging. Their duties as tractors were limited to hauling heavy loads on the road and to winching cable-pulled implements backwards and forwards across the fields. A Victorian traction-engine by Fodens is shown in *photo 1*.

The comparative light weight of petrol-engined vehicles meant that direct ploughing was feasible, and from around 1890 a number of primitive agricultural tractors appeared, notably in the USA where the farms were large enough to bear the high capital cost and risk of the new mechanization. Typical of these early machines was the Otto Gasoline Tractor, made in 1894 in Philadelphia by relatives of the founder of the German Deutz company. An example of this 26-bhp machine, which weighed 5.4 tons, is shown in *photo 2*. A number of firms that were to become synonymous with tractors such as Case, and the Waterloo Gasoline Engine Traction Company (the forerunner to John Deere's tractors) began development of these internal combustion-engined machines in the early 1890s. Case made steam traction-engines from 1876 and their first internal combustion-engined tractor of 1892 is shown in *photo 3*. Among the first in the world to enter series production was the Hart-Parr in 1902, a firm taken over by Oliver in 1929.

Photo 2

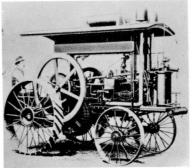

Photo 3

Photo 4

Photo 1

In the USA these new tractors tended to be large so that they could replace whole teams of horses. However, in Europe, they were usually more compact like the Ivel and the Saunderson, introduced in Britain in 1902, though Petter had built a prototype as early as 1892. An Ivel on test in 1902 is shown in *photo 4*. It had an 18/22 hp engine, weighed 1½ tons and had been developed by Daniel Albone since 1897. *Photo 5* shows a German equivalent, the 1907 Deutzer Pfluglokomotive, which had a 5 km/h top speed and a weight of 3 metric tons.

International Harvester in the USA made a friction drive tractor in 1905, and in 1910 introduced their famous internal combustion-engined Mogul range, which embraced 8 to 60 hp models. Shown in *photo 6* is their 15/30 model. Machines of this size naturally tended to sink in soft mud, and in 1904 Holt made the world's first practical crawler tractor to overcome this drawback. In the following year Richard Hornsby, in England, who had been building large oil-engined tractors since 1896, mounted one on tracks to make the first practical internal combustion-engined crawler. He also built the 1910 80 hp steam-driven monster shown in *photo 7*, which spent many years hauling heavy loads in Canada.

Typical of the large oil-engined tractors produced on the European mainland in 1913 was the Munktell shown in *photo 8*. It was designed to replace steam traction-engines by a well-known Swedish locomotive-building company. Its successor, the Bolinder-Munktell Company, was bought by Volvo in 1950.

The most significant event in the early history of the tractor was the arrival of the frameless design on the Wallis Cub in the USA in 1912. Until then, all

Photo 7

Photo 5

Photo 6

Photo 8

tractors had been assembled onto conventional chassis, which added unnecessary weight and, as they were generally without suspension and lacked rigidity, they suffered from engine and transmission alignment problems. In the case of a frameless tractor, everything was held rigidly in place by the unit construction of the engine, gearbox and final drive. Whereas the Cub has exposed pinion and ring drive, its smaller sister, the Junior, shown in *photo 9*, had an enclosed rear-axle drive, and is the direct antecedent of the modern tractor. The Wallis became the forerunner of Massey-Harris tractors when its manufacturing rights were bought in 1927 by the famous Canadian company. Not that tractors with frames were immediately made obsolete, as is shown by the line-up of Internationals at the end of the First World War in *photo 10*. The two Juniors in the foreground are followed by three Titans.

The tractor which really popularized the frameless design was the 1917 Fordson (shown in the montage of American Ford tractor models on page 3). Instead of the fabricated hull of the Wallis it was made from castings, and weighed only a little over a ton. Over 6000 were exported to Britain before the end of the First World War, and afterwards Ford captured almost 75% of the American market, producing 100,000 per year in the early twenties, at rock bottom prices. General Motors took over the Sieve Grip Tractor Co. (a 1918 example is shown in *photo 11* which featured a wide rear wheel to reduce ground pressure and to improve the traction) in an effort to compete, but they, and many of their contemporaries, were soon forced to leave the agricultural market by the slump of the early 1920s.

The really big farming jobs continued to be tackled by traction engines through much of the twenties and thirties, though the heyday for their makers ended with the First World War. A typical American engine of 1917, a Gaar-Scott 25/75 hp, followed by a Sawyer-Massey, and now preserved at the Western Development Museum, Saskatoon, is shown in *photo 12*. Gaar-Scott were associated with another famous tractor maker, Rumely, which was acquired by Allis-Chalmers in 1931.

Photo 9

Photo 11

Photo 10

In an attempt to update the old idea of steam-winch ploughing, and to give it a new lease of life in the face of the ever-increasing competition from tractors, McLaren in England made sets of petrol/paraffin self-propelled winch tackle. They failed to stem the move to direct ploughing, however, and of the few made, three are shown in *photo 13*.

In 1889 and 1890, two rival Californian implement-makers—Best and Holt—made steam-tractors and, as already described, the latter made the first successful crawler tractor in 1904. They joined forces in 1908, though Best's son continued to make tractors on his own until 1925, when he merged with Holt to form Caterpillar Tractors. Holt had coined the name Caterpillar for crawlers before 1910, and shown in *photo 14* is one of the last to bear his name—a 1924 2-ton model.

The relatively primitive state of farming and the small individual acreages on the Continent gave many tractor firms there a slow start. However, an event of far-reaching significance in 1922 was the unveiling of the world's first diesel tractor made by Benz, in Germany. (An early example is shown in *photo 15*.) This new type of engine was adopted in the USA and Britain in

Photo 14

Photo 12

Photo 13

Photo 15

1930, but it was not until after the Second World War that diesels finally ousted petrol/paraffin (starting on petrol and running on paraffin) engines from the majority of tractors. Diesels are inherently far more efficient than spark-ignition engines because of their higher compression and operating temperature.

Early tractors had been simple replacements for draught animals, though they could also power stationary machinery if fitted with belt pulleys. A number of self-propelled hay-cutters and other special-purpose machines had been evolved, but it was not until 1924, when the International Farmall became generally available, that a multi-purpose tractor with PTO (power take off) could be bought. In *photo 16* is the F-12, a refined version of the original Farmall, produced through much of the 1930s.

Photo 16

Another of the new breed of general-purpose tractors was the 1933 Model A, John Deere, shown in *photo 17*. Like most John Deeres for thirty years it featured a horizontal engine and was closely related to the first John Deere tractor introduced in 1923. John Deere had owned the pioneer Waterloo Gasoline Engine Traction Co. since 1918, and had continued for a time its popular Waterloo Boy tractor (known in Britain as the Overtime).

Though motor-cultivators and small garden and horticultural tractors are outside the scope of this book, a number of large two-wheel tractors were made in the USA and Europe before and after the First World War. Shown in *photo 18* is a 1919 Fowler Motor Plough from a range which, by 1923, encompassed 16 to 50 hp two-wheelers. From early success with steam ploughing engines, Fowler went on to make motor tillers and crawler tractors, and joined forces with Marshall at the end of the Second World War.

Typical of Continental tractor practice in the late twenties is the Landini shown in *photo 19*. Fiat, the principal Italian producer, had made only 263 tractors in 1919 and Landini seldom exceeded 200 tractors per year, demonstrating the far more backward state of mechanized farming in Italy and many other European countries when compared with North America.

The makers of the Twin City were one of several farm machinery firms to merge in 1929 in the USA to form Minneapolis-Moline. A Twin City is shown in *photo 20* and had a 12/20 hp engine. American tractors tended to be rated in terms of plough capacity rather than horsepower, e.g. a 2 plough/plow (furrow) tractor. When horsepower was quoted, the smaller figure related to drawbar horsepower, and the larger to belt horsepower, the latter figure being closer to the net output quoted by many European makers. Nowadays, American tractors are usually rated in terms of PTO horsepower.

Photo 18

Photo 19

Photo 17

Photo 20

Photo 21

Photo 22

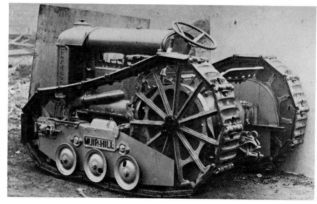

Photo 23

Photo 24

Photo 21 shows the first diesel tractor produced in Italy in 1927, some five years after the first successful Benz diesel tractor ran in Germany. It was made by Francesco Cassani, and had a 40 bhp 2-cylinder engine. He went on to found the makers of SAME tractors.

As well as their unconventional Farmall, International made their first unit-built (frameless) machines, the 15/30 and 10/20 in 1921 and 1922 respectively. Both were well liked, though considerably more expensive than the Fordson; over 200,000 of the smaller model, shown in *photo 22*, were made in its eighteen-year production run.

Over the years Ford tractors have provided a popular basis for all sorts of special-purpose farm machines. Among the earliest in England was the Muir-Hill crawler conversion in 1933, shown in *photo 23*. Nowadays Ford-based crawlers are unusual, though 4 × 4 tractors with Ford components by County, Roadless and Muir-Hill have largely replaced them.

A logical way to get maximum traction without resorting to tracks is all-wheel drive, and 4 × 4 machines have been made for well over fifty years. However, the first competitively priced and widely available 4 × 4 tractor was the Massey-Harris General Purpose in 1930, *photo 24*. It was made for a number of years, but the idea lapsed until the higher horsepowers of the past twenty years made it a necessity once more. Of even greater importance to the development of the tractor was the adoption of pneumatic tyres by Allis-Chalmers in 1932, and by most other American makers soon afterwards. Experiments had been carried out with truck and aircraft tyres before Firestone took the plunge and developed the well-known herring-bone pattern traction tyre. In *photo 25* an Allis-Chalmers Model U, on pneumatic tyres, is shown towing an International combine. To publicize the new ability to travel at speed on the road, and yet still be able to obtain much of the grip of a spadelug wheel, Allis-Chalmers geared up a Model U to attain 64 mph in 1933, while a more standard one averaged $17\frac{1}{2}$ mph for five hours.

Of even more significance was the invention of the three-point linkage with draft control, which is a feature of nearly all today's tractors. It owes its

Photo 25

Photo 26

origin to a talented Ulster engineer named Harry Ferguson, who regarded the primitive tractors of the 1920s as cumbersome, heavy, and only a little more practical than draught animals. The old idea with tractors was to add more weight to the driving wheels to obtain traction, but Ferguson decided that what was needed was a lightweight, and therefore potentially cheaper machine that would bring mechanization to smaller farms around the world, and which would act as a power source for all sorts of implements attached directly to it, and not simply dragged along by it. The two apparently incompatible ideals of good traction and light weight were to be achieved by a scientifically designed attachment point which transferred the weight and resistance of the implement connected to it to a point in front of the back axle. It overcame any tendency to make the tractor rear up by automatically transferring weight that was excess to traction requirements to the front axle. The first prototype, the Ferguson 'Black Tractor' of 1933, with Hercules engine, is shown in *photo 26*.

One major drawback with the early development of the idea, which was eventually overcome by the Ferguson System, was that the mounted implement would tend to dig in deeper if the front wheels went over a bump or would surface if they went into a hollow. To avoid this, Ferguson developed his Draft Control System which, with a sensing unit connected to the hydraulic pump in the lifting linkage, automatically kept the implement at a pre-ordained depth. It could be overridden by the driver if there were major variations in soil conditions in a given field, but normally required no attention at all. Draft Control is explained in diagrammatic form by courtesy of John Deere on the facing page.

David Brown made the production version of the tractor for Harry Ferguson from 1936 to 1939, and when Ferguson took his system to Ford in America in 1939, David Brown introduced their own first tractor, the VAK 1, shown in *photo 27*, which of course incorporated many of the features learned with Ferguson. Though Ferguson perfected the implement lift, hand- or engine-driven lifts had existed on a few tractors from the early years of the century, though until the Ferguson System tractor was developed, most

Photo 27

Photo 28

farmers had been content simply to tow wheeled implements.

Despite this British development, most large-scale tractor use took place in North America, particularly in the vast grain belt, and in *photo 28* can be seen a team of Massey-Harris tractors, developed from the old Wallis mentioned earlier, towing one-way disc ploughs. Massey-Harris and Ferguson eventually merged in 1953 to form Massey-Ferguson.

From the 1920s most tractor makers settled for four-cylinder engines, though there were those who favoured singles and twins as well as a few big tractors with six-cylinder engines. One of the first popular and relatively compact tractors to feature six-cylinders was the Oliver 70 in 1935. It is shown in *photo 29* and was one of the first tractors to hide its utilitarian shape under stylish sheet metal. This streamlined look was taken still further in 1940 when the last vestiges of its radiator were faired-in. Oliver and Minneapolis-Moline, who introduced an optional modern-style driver's cab at the end of the 1930s (a wartime GTA model is shown in *photo 30*) are now owned by White Farm Equipment. Another manufacturer to be absorbed into this firm was Cletrac, who were taken over by Oliver in 1944 and who continued to make crawlers until 1965, when 4×4 machines replaced them. After Caterpillar, Cletrac was probably the best-known name in agricultural crawlers in the 1920s–40s. An example of one at work ploughing, during the Second World War, is given in *photo 31*.

Another American firm with a long agricultural history is Case, whose 1892 tractor was shown in *photo 3* (page 4). They bought the makers of Emerson-Brantingham and Rock Island tractors in 1928 and 1937 respectively, and in 1939 introduced their own first streamlined tractor range, of which the DEX model is shown with a reaper in *photo 32*.

A drawback with the central driving position on tractors is that hoeing, or other intricate rowcrop work on a front or mid-mounted tool bar is partially obscured by the engine cover. This was overcome on the International Farmall range of 1939 by off-setting the engine and driver to give so-called Culti-Vision, shown in *photo 33*.

At various times attempts were made to persuade tractors to run on indigenous fuels. This was particularly so during the First and Second World Wars when imported petroleum was scarce in Europe. Several firms tried

Photo 30

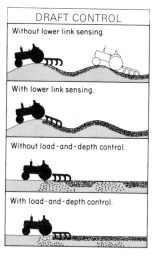

DRAFT CONTROL

Without lower link sensing.

With lower link sensing.

Without load-and-depth control.

With load-and-depth control.

Photo 31

Photo 33

Photo 29

Photo 32

Photo 34

Photo 35

Photo 36

tractors run on gas, which was produced by combustion in a plant on the machine. Shown in *photo 34* is one such machine, a Fendt diesel converted for producer gas. Apart from its fuel, it typifies the continental tractor of the forties and fifties and, indeed, more recent years. Many farms are still small family-run affairs where the complex and sophisticated tractors of today are eschewed in favour of more simple tow-tractors which can also do such jobs as haymaking, with attached implements. Another independent breed of continental tractor is the compact machine for viticulture.

Single-cylinder tractors continued to be popular in Italy and Germany until comparatively recent years. One keen advocate of single-cylinder engines in Britain was Marshall, who made their first in 1930 and continued to offer refined versions right up to 1957, some of the latter as crawlers produced by their associates, Fowler. In *photo 35* their Field Marshall Series I of 1945 is shown. Though single-cylinder machines could accomplish most farm jobs, they were particularly liked for their ability to power stationary equipment and were economical and appropriate replacements for the old stationary barn engines.

Ferguson System tractors were produced by Ford in America from 1939 to 1946, and then Harry Ferguson set up a firm in association with the Standard Motor Company of Coventry to make his tractors in England. *Photo 36* shows a 1947 Ferguson TEA petrol-engined model with Harry Ferguson at the wheel. It was joined by the TED vaporizing oil model in 1949, and from 1952 Perkins diesel conversions were available. The Perkins Company was acquired by Massey-Ferguson in 1959.

After sixteen years production the Fordson N was replaced in Britain by the E27N (shown in *photo 37*) in 1945, which used a similar engine and many other parts from the N, but had larger wheels and a three-point hydraulic lift.

Photo 37

It was not until the thirties that tractors had become an everyday part of farming life, and the Second World War which followed caused a vast expansion in land clearance and mechanized farming to feed blockaded Europe. Following the war, several new tractor manufacturers appeared in the industrialized countries, one of the most significant being the motor tycoon William Morris (by then Lord Nuffield) with his Nuffield tractor in 1948. A tricycle rowcrop version is shown in *photo 38*. The Nuffield was one of the first tractors to have five forward gears in place of the prevalent three or four used by most other manufacturers. Indeed, until the twenties a single forward and reverse gear were commonplace, and two or three forward gears were considered adequate for many years afterwards. With a dual-range gearbox, the Nuffield, which became the Leyland tractor in 1969, acquired ten forward speeds. The past twenty years has seen all tractor-makers adopt multi-speed transmissions to give the best working speed at optimum engine revs for every type of job from $\frac{1}{4}$ mph planting to 20 mph road work. They are often based on a three-, four- or five-speed unit, with epicyclic splitters to multiply the ratios available by two, three or four times. Other developments have provided synchromesh or other means of making easy, on-the-move gear changes.

The USA had always out-produced the other tractor-making nations, though Britain came second, primarily because of the Fordsons produced at Dagenham from the early thirties; and afterwards because of the Ferguson, David Brown and Nuffield in addition. After the war, the American giants looked around for means of expansion, and International, Caterpillar, Allis-Chalmers, and of course, Massey-Harris, soon started to produce tractors in Britain. International were first in 1949, and in 1956 they introduced their first wholly British designed and made tractor, the B-250; before that, they had made tractors with a number of local features. One of these was the

Photo 39

Photo 40

super BMD, shown in *photo 39*. It appeared in 1953 with a 43/48 hp diesel engine. Allis-Chalmers also built their B model in Britain and offered a wide range of crawlers with GMC 2-stroke diesel engines. An HD5 with 3-cylinder engine and 5-speed gearbox is shown in *photo 40*. Some, primarily for the construction industry, were unusual in having infinitely variable torque converter transmissions (a feature which has only recently become practical on tractors—the International 574 Hydro being an example of a tractor with infinitely variable hydrostatic transmission).

Photo 38

As well as new manufacturers in existing tractor-producing areas, several countries that had previously relied on animal power, plus the occasional imported machine, started their own tractor industries. Finland had made around 100 Kullervo tractors in 1918–24, but the Valmet which appeared in 1953 was far more successful. In *photo 41* a 1955 example of their four-cylinder 20 hp petrol/paraffin model 20 is shown.

Larger farms and reduced manpower have meant that big tractors able to cultivate the largest possible area in each pass have grown in importance. *Photo 42* shows John Deere's largest tractor in 1949, and their first with a diesel engine. It is a model R developing 43 PTO hp.

More engine-power increased the problems of transmitting it to the ground without excessive wheelspin, and for many of the larger jobs, particularly where minimal panning of the ground was essential, the crawler reigned, and indeed still reigns supreme. An example of a 55 hp Fiat is shown at work in *photo 43*, in 1952. This tractor, and several of its continental contemporaries, favoured steering-wheel control instead of the more usual lever-operated steering clutches.

Four-wheel drive was once more examined and in 1954 County introduced an unusual machine combining the skid-steering of a crawler, and four equal-sized tractor tyres to give extra mobility. It was based on the Fordson Major introduced at the end of 1951 and is shown in *photo 44*. In 1960 County adopted more normal pivoting front wheels. Another ingenious system to give maximum traction and extra horsepower was to link two Fordson tractors and give them pivot-steering. The resulting Doe Triple D was made in Britain for some years from 1957 and is shown in *photo 45*.

Photo 42

Photo 43

Photo 41

Photo 44

Pivot-steering is now widely used on large 4 × 4 single-engine tractors, while a similar system to the Doe has been adopted by Steiger to make their 18-ton 650-bhp Twin Panther. Among the earliest big horsepower 4 × 4 machines was the MRS, developed for the alluvial plains of the Mississippi. Tractors of up to 220 bhp were available from MRS in 1962 and all had four-wheel steering. An example is shown in *photo 46*. As well as tractors with 4 × 4 and equal-sized wheels, driven front axles were fitted to conventionally-shaped tractors in the sixties by a number of firms, and an unusual example, the 67 hp Bührer from Switzerland is shown in *photo 47*.

Perhaps epitomizing the multi-national nature of the tractor industry nowadays is the Oliver 500, shown in *photo 48*. This machine, and the 600, were available in the early 1960s and both were made for Oliver by David Brown, being their DB 880 and 990 models, with minor restyling. Fiat now supply White/Oliver with tractors under a similar arrangement. Meanwhile David Brown was acquired by Case in 1972.

Other North American tractor firms have established tractor plants in numerous developing nations and have also bought existing tractor manufacturers. Examples are John Deere owning Chamberlain in Australia, and Massey-Ferguson owning Landini in Italy. These big firms are taking over an ever larger share of the tractor market, though there is still room for over fifty small specialist firms, plus of course the giants behind the Iron Curtain. In 1960 eleven tractor manufacturers, Massey-Ferguson, IHC (International), Ford, Fiat, Deutz, John Deere, SAME, Renault, David Brown, Fendt and Zetor had 64·7% of the tractor market. By the end of 1975 the percentage had increased to 82·1, and over 40% of sales were shared between the three multi-national giants, Massey-Ferguson, IHC and Ford. These figures come from Ford, who also note that whereas the average horsepower of a tractor sold in Europe in 1968 was 47·8, it became 63·8 in 1975, and is expected to reach 71 by 1980. In North America almost 60% of sales are over 90 hp.

Nowadays many countries require the fitment of safety cabs or cages to tractors to protect the driver in the event of the vehicle turning over sideways, or tipping over backwards. In addition, some countries now require soundproof cabs to minimize ear damage. The resulting tractors would be unrecognizable to the pioneers of eighty years ago in terms of both appearance and capabilities.

Photo 45

Photo 46

Photo 47

Photo 48

Adriatica, Italy
White sheet metal and wheels: green engine and transmission

Adriatica started to produce agricultural equipment in the mid-fifties and now make small diesel engines, pumps, motor-cultivators, scythes and binders, as well as two- and four-wheel drive tractors of up to 30 bhp, with up to 50 bhp under development. The 4 × 4 tractors have equal-sized wheels all round and, in common with the 4 × 2 model, can be supplied with powered-axle trailers.

Aebi, Switzerland
Red with white wheels

Aebi have concentrated on special tractors for hill farmers and local authorities in their native country for over twenty-five years. To cope with difficult operating angles their latest Terratrac TT77 is equipped with four-wheel drive, and locking front and rear differentials. Its low profile and wide wheels enable it to work across slopes impossible for more conventional machines. It can be supplied with front and rear PTO and three-point linkage.

Agria, West Germany
Red sheet metal and wheels: off-white engine and transmission

Agria have made cultivators and implements for some thirty years and now produce mowers, cultivators and small garden and horticultural 4 × 2 tractors. In addition, they make a larger 4 × 4 machine for special agricultural purposes and vineyard work.

Aebi The Terratrac TT77 is powered by a Perkins 43 DIN hp diesel engine, and six forward and six reverse gears are provided. Front-wheel drive can be disengaged for road work and up to 25 km/h is possible. The frame pivots in order to keep all wheels in equal contact with the ground.

Adriatica The Minitractor has an 817 cc, four-stroke, single-cylinder Lombardini diesel engine developing 18/21 bhp. It has four forward and two reverse gears. Three-point linkage and multi-speed PTOs are fitted, as well as differential lock and electric starting.

Agria 6700 is a pivot-steer 4 × 4 tractor with two-cylinder air-cooled diesel of 30 SAE hp. Eight forward and four reverse gears give up to 20·1 km/h, and three-point linkage and two-speed PTO are fitted.

Agrifull, Italy
Pale green with white wheels

Agrifull tractors are made at the factory of the hundred-year-old Toselli agricultural machinery company. Agrifull is a recently-formed group which offers a wide range of agricultural equipment and includes SAIMM, makers of balers and forage-harvesters, and Gherardi, makers of ploughs and tilling machinery. Toselli produces small-wheeled and crawler vineyard tractors, as well as the Agrifull tractor range, the 35-bhp Pony, 45-bhp Sprint, 47-bhp Jolly, 60-bhp Derby, 70-bhp Griso, 80-bhp Tornado, 90-bhp Rodeo and 115-bhp Pinto, all with two- or four-wheel drive and VM air-cooled diesel engines.

Agrifull Tornado 80 has a VM 3808 cc four-cylinder 77-bhp diesel engine, which is also used in turbocharged form in the Rodeo 90. The gearbox provides twelve forward and four reverse speeds up to 24·5 km/h. Creeper gears can be added, as can 1000 rpm PTO. Ground speed and 540 rpm PTO are standard.

Agrifull The 345 Vigneto Sprint has a VM three-cylinder diesel engine of 50 SAE hp, six forward and two reverse gears, plus optional three forward and one reverse creeper gears. 540 rpm and ground-speed PTO are fitted. It is a compact model with two- or four-wheel drive for vineyard and orchard use.

Allis-Chalmers, USA
Orange with white wheels

Founded in 1847 as millstone suppliers, Allis-Chalmers made their first tractor in 1913. In 1929 they joined a short-lived manufacturing co-operative to make the United tractor, forerunner of the famous Allis-Chalmers model U. The crawler version of this was the model M, named in honour of the Monarch Tractor Co which had been acquired in 1928 and which made an experimental diesel crawler in 1930. Allis-Chalmers also bought the Advance-Rumely tractor firm in 1931. The model U was a pioneer user of pneumatic tyres in 1932, and in 1934 it was joined by the general-purpose model WC, one of the first tractors designed from scratch for pneumatic tyres.

Allis-Chalmers 185 has a six-cylinder 301 cu. in. 75 PTO hp diesel engine, and eight forward and two reverse gears giving up to 17 mph. 540 rpm PTO is standard and 540/1000 rpm optional. Power-adjusted rear track width and 'Traction Booster' hydraulic drawbar are fitted.

Allis-Chalmers The 7080 has a 426 cu. in. (6980 cc) six-cylinder diesel which develops 181·5 PTO hp in this application but, with varying degrees of turbocharge and other details, powers the 136 PTO hp 7040, the 161·5 PTO hp 7060 and the 4 × 4 7580. The 7080 has 1000 rpm PTO and five forward and four reverse gears, with four ranges giving twenty forward ratios.

Allis-Chalmers The 7580 has a six-cylinder 6980 cc turbocharged and intercooled diesel developing 185 PTO hp (222 SAE hp), has 20 forward and 4 reverse gears giving up to 19·5 mph and 1000 rpm PTO. Pivot-steering gives 34-foot turning circle. Three-point linkage is available.

Allis-Chalmers crawlers later received GMC two-stroke diesel engines and in the forties some of these were the first to use torque-converter transmission.

Allis-Chalmers tractors were popular in Britain and for a time in the fifties/sixties their little model B (introduced in the USA in 1938) and modified British successors were made in Lincolnshire. Allis-Chalmers crawler tractors for the construction industry are now made by a jointly-owned company, Fiat-Allis, but Allis-Chalmers themselves make small garden tractors and 62 to 185 PTO hp wheeled farm tractors, the largest replacing a model previously made for them by Steiger. The smaller A-C 40 and 50 hp models are produced for them by Fiat.

Aveling Marshall is available with 100-bhp Perkins or 105-bhp Ford six-cylinder diesel engines, with designations AM100 and AM105. They have five forward and three reverse gears, and drawbar pull is approximately 20,000 lb. Three-point linkage and PTO are available.

Aveling Marshall, UK
Buttercup yellow

Marshall made steam agricultural equipment from 1876. In 1930 they introduced their single-cylinder, two-stroke diesel tractors which, with gradual modifications (and the name Field-Marshall) continued until 1957. They were associated in the 1940s with Fowlers, who produced a crawler version of the Marshall, and in 1957 the Track-Marshall appeared, as well as the final wheeled Marshall, the Leyland-engined MP6 export tractor. Marshall later acquired the makers of Bristol crawlers and, in 1976, were themselves bought by Leyland. Their tractors have now been renamed Aveling Marshall, after Aveling-Barford, the well-known construction machinery firm in the Leyland group.

Ballu, France

A small French maker of vineyard tractors.

Barreiros, Spain
Red with grey engine and transmission

Barreiros began to produce commercial vehicles in 1954 and later added tractors as well. Following its acquisition by the American firm Chrysler, it changed its name to Chrysler España in 1970, though tractors and some other vehicles retain their old name.

Belarus MTZ 52 has four-cylinder 70 SAE hp (58 PTO hp) diesel and front-axle drive automatically engaged when rear wheels slip by more than five per cent. The high-mounted, reduction front axle gives 58 cm crop clearance, and the gearbox provides nine forward and two reverse ratios through one lever.

Barreiros 4000 has a three-cylinder 2505 cc diesel engine developing 45 bhp (40 PTO hp at 540 rpm). It has five forward and one reverse gears, or optionally ten plus two.

Belarus, USSR
Red with white wheels

The Minsk factory was started in 1950 and produced its millionth tractor in 1972. It makes a variety of models from the MTZ 50 to 80, and these are available with 4 × 4 (MTZ 52 to 82). Tractors from Minsk are called Belarus after the Russian province in which they are made, and this name is given to tractors from other Soviet factories in some export territories, notably Britain.

Bertolini, Italy
White wheels and engine cover: pale blue elsewhere

Bertolini started in 1918 by making pumps and agricultural spraying equipment, and later developed motor-cultivators and hay-cutters. They now make a wide range of cultivators, hay-making machines, agricultural load-carriers and small tractors. The latter are powered by engines of up to 48 bhp, in 4 × 4 (equal-sized wheels) models, and 36 bhp in 4 × 2 models.

Bertolini 530 model can have 24, 28 or 32 bhp, two-cylinder or 36-bhp three-cylinder diesel engines. Six forward and three reverse gears are provided. Three-point linkage is available.

Blank, West Germany
Black and white

Karl Blank has produced compact tractors since 1951 for rowcrop and vineyard work. The firm concentrated on miniature crawlers for many years, but in 1966 added four-wheel drive Mustang models. Blank now produce 14,30 and 55-bhp versions of crawler, conventional two-wheel drive, and Mustang 4 × 4 tractors, as well as stilt tractors with 35-bhp engines for high-clearance work.

Bobard, France
Yellow wheels and engine cover, otherwise blue: sometimes blue all over apart from red wheels

Bobard have made crop-spraying equipment since 1927 and in 1954 introduced their first tractor, a special rowcrop machine. They now make 700 tractors per year, primarily for cultivating and spraying tall crops and vines. These include conventional high-clearance tractors with three-cylinder 55-bhp, and four-cylinder 65-bhp Perkins diesels, as well as the ingenious Poly Bob, which in its Alsace version can clear crops up to 2·5 metres high.

Blank Sharing some 70 per cent of its components with the largest Mustang is the V 355 crawler. It has eight forward gears and a top speed of 12 km/h.

Bobard The B45 Poly Bob has two equal-sized driven and steered wheels placed in line, and steadying wheels on either side adjustable for row width and for keeping the machine vertical when working across slopes. Power comes from a two-litre Indenor diesel, and there is a two-range gearbox giving eight forward and two reverse gears. Top speed is 23 km/h and towing force six tonnes.

Blank Mustang 355 has three-cylinder 55 DIN hp air-cooled diesel, and ten forward, two reverse speed gearbox. Hydrostatic steering is standard and a 540/1050 rpm PTO is fitted.

Bolgar TL 30A is a vineyard model with a total width of only 1 metre. It has a 35-bhp three-cylinder diesel of 2965 cc capacity, and five forward and one reverse gears. Its three-point linkage gives a lift of up to 660 kg.

Bolgar, Bulgaria
Beige mechanical parts with yellow elsewhere

Bulgarian agricultural crawlers are sold under the name Bolgar and cover medium horsepower models for general farm duties (notably the T-54V model of 60 bhp) and smaller machines for vineyard use.

Bratstvo, Yugoslavia
Orange with white cab roof

Bratstvo are primarily makers of steel forgings and hand tools. They make axles, crankshafts and other engine parts for the Yugoslavian motor industry, and for such firms as Fiat and Mercedes-Benz. They also make farm implements and BNT crawler tractors.

Bührer, Switzerland
Green and red

Founded in 1879, Bührer produced their first tractor in 1929 and commenced diesel tractor production in 1941. They developed a three-range transmission in 1954 and, ten years later, improved it with their Tractospeed gearbox to give fully manual on-the-move changes to fifteen forward and three reverse gears. In recent years Chrysler, Mercedes, Perkins, Ford and Bührer-engined models have been offered, some with four-wheel drive; by 1971 the company had sold a total of 20,000 tractors. They are now members of the Rapid Group, which makes agricultural machinery and motor-cultivators, and produce Switzerland's only large horsepower tractors. In 1976 an entirely restyled range, incorporating Tractospeed, was announced covering 4 × 2 and 4 × 4 models of 45 to 135 DIN hp.

Bratstvo BNT-90 has a Famos Sarajevo 90-bhp six-cylinder diesel engine and seven forward and one reverse gears. The 70-bhp four-cylinder BNT-70, with five forward speeds, is also available.

Bührer 685 has a six-cylinder diesel engine developing 85 bhp. Tractospeed gearbox gives fifteen forward and three reverse gears. This is the largest Bührer with two-wheel drive, the 6105 and 6135 being 4 × 4 models.

Carraro, Italy
Red with olive green axles, engine and transmission

Carraro make three-cylinder 50- and 69-bhp crawlers and two- and four-wheel drive tractors of up to 69 bhp. In 1972 statistics, they were the third largest supplier of 4 × 4 tractors to Italian farms after Fiat and SAME. They also supply 4 × 4 tractors and front drive axles to Renault in France.

Case, USA
White with orange engine and transmission, and orange and silver wheels

Case's roots go back to 1842 and for many years they were the largest maker of steam traction-engines in America. In 1892 they turned their attention to internal combustion-engined tractors, and a feature of many of their later tractors was a vertical engine mounted horizontally in front of the driving axle. More conventional layout followed with such well-remembered models as the L and D ranges of the thirties and forties.

In their long history, Case have taken over various tractor firms, including Emerson-Brantingham and Rock Island, and in 1972 their parent company, Tenneco, acquired the tractor interests of the British David Brown firm who now make many of the medium-sized Case models sold in the USA. The current Case range starts at 8–16.5 hp miniature tractors and extends to the giant 2870 four-wheel drive model powered by a Brazilian-built and Swedish-designed Scania DS11 turbocharged diesel.

Case Agri King 970 has a six-cylinder 93 PTO hp diesel of larger capacity (401 cu. in.) than most other tractors in its horsepower class. Its drawbar pull is over 11,000 lb, and eight-speed dual range or twelve-speed four range transmission is available. Agri Kings come in six horsepower sizes, from 80 to 180 PTO hp.

Carraro 702 is the two-wheel drive version of the 4 × 4 704 model. It has a three-cylinder 4250 cc air-cooled 69-bhp diesel engine, and sixteen forward and four reverse gears. Hydraulic linkage gives 3472 kg lift and a 540 rpm PTO is fitted.

Case giant 4 × 4s differ from most other American machines of their type in having independent steering axles rather than centre pivot-steer. As a result, they can be steered by front wheels alone, or by the rear wheels, or a combination of the two. Here a 2670 demonstrates how it avoids side-slip on a hill by steering crabwise. It has a turbocharged 221 PTO hp Case six-cylinder diesel, and three forward gears in each of four ranges.

CAST, Italy

CAST make the familiar Italian type of small four-wheel drive tractors which, however, differ from most of their competitors in having four-wheel kingpin, as opposed to pivot steering. An unusual feature is that the seat can be placed on either side of the steering-column for driving convenience in each direction. 14-, 20- and 28-bhp models are offered.

Caterpillar, USA
Yellow

Daniel Best and Benjamin Holt owned rival agricultural machinery businesses in California, and in 1889 and 1890 respectively built their first steam tractors. These vast machines tended to sink into the ground, and later models were fitted with giant wheels to reduce ground pressure. Taking the idea a step further, Holt fitted his tractor number 77 with creeper tracks in 1904 and soon coined the name Caterpillar for the new type of tractor. He registered the name in 1910. Petrol-engined crawlers were built by Holt from 1906, and in 1908 Best sold out to Holt, though his son made his own Best tractors until he, too, joined forces with Holt in 1925 to create the Caterpillar Tractor Co. In 1931 they made one of the world's first diesel crawlers.

Until the advent of large 4 × 4 tractors, Caterpillars were among the best-known machines for the bigger farm tasks, and though crawlers of up to 820 bhp for the construction industry now predominate, Caterpillar continue to make 62- to 200-bhp models (D3 to D7) for farm use, especially where low ground pressure and maximum traction is essential. Their tractors are made in a number of plants around the world including Japan (Mitsubishi) and Britain, where Caterpillar started their first overseas subsidiary in 1950.

CAST 430 L has a two-cylinder Slanzi 1330 cc diesel engine with air-cooling which develops 28 bhp. It has six gears in either direction, hydraulic lift and ground speed, and 540 rpm PTO.

CBT, Brazil
Yellow with white wheels and radiator guard

CBT started in 1960 by producing Oliver 950s under licence. After 200 had been built, the tractor was redesigned by CBT and equipped with a Mercedes-Benz diesel engine. From 1968 Perkins engines were also used, although the firm has future plans to make its own engines. CBT make approximately 12,000 tractors per year and have plans to increase this to 100 per day. All models are frame-built and range from 55 to 120 bhp.

Caterpillar D4 has a four-cylinder, seven-litre 90-bhp diesel engine, and five forward gears giving up to 4·6 mph and 14,785 lb drawbar pull. Three-point linkage is standard on agricultural models.

CBT 1000 has a 3·33-litre four-cylinder Perkins diesel engine developing 61 bhp. It has six forward and two reverse gears. 540 rpm PTO is available and three-point linkage standard.

CBT 1105 has a six-cylinder Mercedes-Benz diesel engine of 5675 cc capacity producing 105 bhp. It has six forward and two reverse gears. Hydraulic system and 540/1000 rpm PTO are optionally available.

Chamberlain, Australia
Yellow and black

The first Chamberlain tractor was a 40 drawbar hp twin-cylinder kerosene-engine machine in 1949, and in the 1950s 60-, 70- and 90-bhp diesel tractors and agricultural implements were developed. Chamberlain recently joined forces with John Deere and now offer these tractors alongside their own yellow Sedan range of 73–124 SAE hp John Deere-engined tractors. To suit Australian requirements they have drawbars as standard equipment with PTOs, though three-point linkage is available on the two smallest adjustable track models.

Corghi, Italy

Corghi offer standard and vineyard width two-wheel drive 14- and 20-bhp Slanzi-engined models.

County, UK
Blue with white cab and wheels (apart from blue centres)

Founded in 1929, County were well known for their truck conversions, notably in turning Ford four-wheelers into six-wheelers. In 1948 they started to make crawler versions of the Fordson Major and from this developed one of the first four-wheel drive tractors with equal-sized pneumatic tyres all round (in 1954). This was initially skid-steered, like the crawlers it had been designed to replace in the sugar-cane industry. In 1960 more conventional king-pin steering was adopted, and in 1964 crawlers were finally discontinued.

Around 40,000 County tractors have been produced with examples exported to 150 countries. This firm now makes High-Drive crop-clearance tractors, and 4 × 4 tractors with both small front wheels and equal-sized wheels, some of the latter with forward control, and all based on Ford components.

Chamberlain Smallest in the range is the 3380 with four-cylinder 73 SAE hp (68 PTO hp) John Deere diesel engine. The constant mesh Hi-Lo transmission provides twelve forward and four reverse gears, and final drive is planetary. Top speed is 21 mph, and the cab and contents are isolated from the rest of the tractor by four rubber cones.

Corghi CD 23/t has a two-cylinder 1020 cc Slanzi diesel engine developing 20 bhp. It has air-cooling. Six forward and two reverse gears are provided and 540 rpm PTO is standard. Three-point linkage is available.

County The largest model is the 1454, which has a turbocharged version of the 6571 cc six-cylinder Ford diesel found in the 1254. DIN hp outputs are respectively 138 and 118.

Drive to each front wheel is by individual shafts and one lockable differential covers all wheels. Five position, dual range, dual power transmission give sixteen forward and four reverse gears.

County The Forward Control tractor has a six-cylinder 5948 cc Ford diesel engine developing 102 bhp. Dual range gearbox gives eight forward and two reverse gears and three-point linkage and 540 rpm PTO are fitted. As well as normal 4 × 4 tractor capabilities, this machine can carry a load of 16,000 lb.

David Brown The 1410 is the largest of this firm's tractors and is available with two- or, as shown here, four-wheel drive. The engine is a turbocharged 3594 cc DB unit developing 91 DIN hp (81 PTO hp) and it has a synchromesh gearbox giving three forward and one reverse gear in each of four ranges.

David Brown, UK
White with orange wheels, engine and transmission

Famed for their gear-making and general engineering, David Brown supplied parts for the prototype tractors that Harry Ferguson developed in the mid-thirties. When Ferguson looked for a firm to make his first production tractors, he chose David Brown, and they built about 1500 between 1936/39 and then introduced their own VAK 1 model in 1939. This became the familiar post-war Cropmaster.

The 900 series tractors appeared in 1956, and from 1959 featured Implematic controls which could handle depth-wheels or draft-controlled implements with equal ease. In 1965 the old red DB livery was changed for

white and brown, and following the acquisition of David Brown's tractor interests by the owners of JI Case in 1972, a joint colour scheme of red (Case colour) and white was adopted in the following year. David Browns are now sold in certain countries, including the USA, under the Case name, and their range covers tractors of 48 to 91 DIN hp.

David Brown The 1212 has a similar four-cylinder DB engine to the 1410 and its Hydra-Shift sister, the 1412, but unlike them does not have a turbocharger. It develops 72 DIN hp (65 PTO hp) and has Hydra-Shift transmission, which gives on-the-move clutchless gear changes to any of four ratios within four different ranges (creep, field, road, reverse).

Deere The 3130 tractor has a 99 SAE hp six-cylinder John Deere engine. The transmission provides twelve forward and six reverse gears and incorporates a clutchless Hi-Lo change-ratio within each gear. The example shown has hydrostatic motors powered by the hydraulic system built into each front wheel hub to give four-wheel drive when required, without complex drive shafts and differential.

Deere, USA
Green with yellow wheels and stripe

John Deere was a long-established implement-maker who, in 1918, acquired the manufacturers of the Waterloo Boy tractor, a machine well-known in Britain during the First World War as the Overtime. The first true John Deere tractor appeared in 1923 and, with very few exceptions, all their subsequent tractors had horizontal engines until 1962, when a more conventional vertical layout was adopted and the makers of FWD-Wagner 4 × 4 tractors acquired. John Deere tractors are now produced in the USA as well as Mexico, Argentina, Spain, Iran, Australia and West Germany (in the former factory of the makers of the Lanz Bulldog), and include machines of 53 to 275 hp.

Deere make two pivot-steer 4 × 4 tractors, the 8430 and the 8630 which deliver 215 and 275 bhp (175 and 225 PTO hp) respectively. Both have six-cylinder turbocharged John Deere diesel engines of 7636 and 10,144 cc capacity in each case, and sixteen forward and four reverse gears selected from four forward and one reverse gears, each with Quad-Range to suit PTO work, heavy and light fieldwork and moving between jobs.

Dehondt, France
Red with white wheels and cab

Dehondt make many types of agricultural implement; one of their specialities is front-mounted tool bars for conventional tractors to enable them to complete two cultivation or planting operations in one pass. To give improved operator control over front-mounted implements, Dehondt have developed a range of forward control AUTOtractoMOTRICE tractors of 50 to 120 bhp.

Deere The 4230 has a normally aspirated six-cylinder diesel engine developing 122 bhp. The engine, with different degrees of turbocharging, powers the 149-bhp model 4430 and 177-bhp model 4630, all of which have choice of 8 plus 2 or 13 forward plus 4 reverse gear transmission. The 8 plus 2 4230/4430 can also have 16 forward plus 6 reverse gears Quad Range/8 plus 4 Power Shift.

Dehondt Forward control 85-bhp tractor showing typical front- and rear-mounted implements. Dehondt tractors use a high proportion of International Harvester components and are available with two- or, as shown here, four-wheel drive.

Deutz, West Germany
Lime green with orange wheels and grey engine and transmission

The origins of the company go back to 1864, and in 1876 the founder, N. Otto, produced the world's first four-stroke engine. Dr Diesel worked at Deutz in the 1890s on his famous compression ignition engine, and from 1907 Deutz carried out experiments with tractors. The first production diesel tractor from Deutz was in 1927 and they made lightweight 11 hp machines from 1936. Air-cooled engine production began in 1942 and was adopted by their tractors in 1950. Deutz have owned the makers of Fahr agricultural machinery since 1969 and now make a wide range of 45–160 bhp two- and four-wheel drive tractors, plus the Intrac 4 × 4 forward control tool- and load-carrier. Deutz tractors are made under licence in several other countries including Yugoslavia (by Torpedo) and in South America.

Deutz The D 80 06 has a six-cylinder 5652 cc 80-bhp air-cooled Deutz diesel and choice of up to sixteen forward and seven reverse gears, with synchromesh on the top two gears in two or three ranges. It is available with two- or four-wheel drive; two PTO speeds are standard.

Deutz Intrac 2003 (2003A when 4 × 4) is a multi-purpose farming vehicle with a four-cylinder 3768 cc air-cooled diesel of 72 bhp. Eight forward/four reverse synchromesh gears are provided, plus four additional creeper gears if required. Rear 540/1000 rpm PTO and front 1000 rpm PTO are fitted. Smaller three-cylinder models, and larger ones with equal-sized wheels all round are available.

Deutz The smallest is the 45-bhp three-cylinder air-cooled D 45 06. An eight forward plus two reverse speed transmission is standard, but 8/4 or 12/4 speeds are optional. 540/1000 rpm PTO is fitted.

Deutz Largest model is the pivot-steer D160 06, with 160-bhp air-cooled six-cylinder diesel engine and equal-sized wheels all round. The model is under development and a prototype is shown.

Dongfeng, China
Red with olive green frame and orange flywheel

Although motor-cultivators are outside the scope of this book, the Dongfeng 12 is included to show Communist China's principal form of mechanized agriculture. The model can be adapted for various types of cultivation and towing. A conventional 35-bhp tractor, based on the Massey-Ferguson 35 of the mid-fifties, the FS 35, is also used in smaller quantities, but at the time of publication it had been temporarily discontinued while modifications were incorporated.

Dongfeng 12 has a hand-started 12-bhp single-cylinder hopper-cooled diesel engine, and six forward and two reverse gears giving up to 15·3 km/h. The operator sits above a jockey wheel, and the flywheel can be used to power belt-driven stationary machinery.

Ebro, Spain   *Light blue and grey*

Founded in 1920 to make Fords in Spain, Motor Iberica was nationalized in 1954 and in 1966 joined forces with the Spanish Massey-Ferguson and Perkins companies. In 1973 it added licence-built Valpadana tractors to its range and a year later started to build FRAT tractors for the Syrian Government at a new factory in Aleppo. In 1975 it acquired the Sema-Renault tractor factory at Burgos to expand production, and now makes 21- to 140-bhp machines.

Ebro 160E has a four-cylinder 50 drawbar horsepower diesel engine of Motor Iberica's own manufacture, and has six forward and two reverse gears. 540 rpm PTO and hydraulic linkage are standard.

Eicher, West Germany
Blue with red wheels and grey engine and transmission

The history of Eicher goes back some 75 years and their first tractor was produced in 1936. In 1970 Massey-Ferguson acquired a 30 per cent stake in the company which now fits some Perkins (M-F owned) diesels in its middle-range models. Eicher make small air-cooled vineyard tractors up to general-purpose 4 × 4 tractors with air-cooled 130 DIN hp six-cylinder diesels of their own manufacture. Many of the intermediate models like the Königs-Tiger (45 DIN hp), Mammut (55 DIN hp) and Büffel (74 DIN hp) are available with two- or four-wheel drive.

Eicher Büffel-Allrad (Buffalo all-wheel drive) has Perkins 74 DIN hp four-cylinder diesel and twelve forward and four reverse gears giving up to 25 km/h.

Eicher Small vineyard tractors come in 30, 34, 42 and 52 DIN hp sizes with two- or three-cylinder forced-draft air-cooling, and with two- or four-wheel drive. Shown is a two-cylinder 3706 A-74 model (with the cages for its cooling fans visible) and four-wheel drive.

Energic, France

Patissier are small French manufacturers of Energic general-purpose tractors.

Eron, Italy

Meroni is a metal-working firm dating from 1800 which now makes small Eron 4 × 4 tractors of the familiar Italian pattern, except that steering is on the front wheels alone.

Fendt, West Germany

Green with red wheels and grey engine and transmission

The Fendt family were farmers and blacksmiths who, in 1928, built a tractor with mounted cutter-bar for their own use and were then asked to make similar machines for neighbouring farmers.

From these small beginnings the privately-owned company now makes around 17,000 tractors per year including vineyard tractors, tool-carriers, the Agrobil-S forage-harvester and ten-tonne load-carrier, as well as an extensive range of general-purpose tractors of 45 to 165 bhp. The engines for many of these are made by MWM; four-wheel drive is available in much of the range and is standard above 120 bhp. An unusual feature of many of the models is independent springing for each front wheel, in addition to the usual central pivot.

Fendt Favorit SL range incorporates a number of interesting technical features including a Turbomatik hydraulic clutch on which all power transmission takes place between two turbine plates that never touch, but rely on liquid between them to lock them smoothly or allow them to freewheel. The synchromesh gearbox gives 16 forward and 7 reverse gears and there is on-the-move 540/1000 rpm PTO selection. The 612 SL (130 bhp) shown shares a similar 6·3 litre six-cylinder diesel with the 610 SL (100 bhp), 611 SL (120 bhp) 614 SL (150 bhp) and 615 SL (165 bhp), except that the last two are supercharged.

Eron D 350 has a two-cylinder air-cooled Vancini diesel of 1728 cc capacity and 33 bhp output. Six forward and two reverse gears give up to 24 km/h. Hydraulic lift and PTO are available.

Fendt make a number of 'One Man System' models able to accomplish the majority of farming jobs by simply substituting equipment on a basic frame. On this F250GT of 45 DIN hp the dropside body can be replaced by seed-drill, liquid tank, front-loader of other implements.

Fiat 1300 can have two- or four- (1300 DT) wheel drive. It has a six-cylinder Fiat/OM 7412 cc diesel developing 150 DIN hp. Twelve forward and four reverse gears are standard, although four additional creeper gears are optionally available. Two-speed independent PTOs are fitted.

Ferrari 75 RS has a two-cylinder air-cooled 30-bhp diesel, and seven forward and three reverse gears. Hydrostatic transmission is available where continuous work at speeds of under 1000 metres per hour is required. Two-speed PTO and hydraulic lift are standard.

Ferrari, Italy
Spruce green with white wheels

Ferrari make 4 × 4 agricultural load-carriers, motor-scythes and cultivators, and compact diesel tractors. These include two-wheel drive 14-bhp machines, and 4 × 4 pivot-steer and front-wheel steer two- and three-cylinder tractors of up to 45 bhp.

Fiat, Italy
Orange with white wheels

Fiat was founded in 1899 and made its first vehicle three years later. Tractor production has grown from 263 in 1919, and 1800 in 1949, to approximately 100,000 per year today. Fiat are now one of the five largest producers of tractors in the West and claim to be the sales leader in 4 × 4 and crawler machines. They have manufacturing arrangements in a number of countries and sell their tractors in France under the name SOMECA. They produce the smaller models in the North American White/Oliver range and have a joint company with Allis-Chalmers called Fiat-Allis making crawler tractors and other machinery for the construction industry. They have owned the pioneer Italian truck and tractor firm, OM, since 1933, who now produce Fiat tractor engines.

Crawlers still account for almost a quarter of tractor sales in Italy (against under one per cent in most non-Mediterranean European countries), and Fiat make a number of crawler models as well as two- and four-wheel drive machines of 28 to 150 bhp.

Fiat The 450 has a three-cylinder 2340 cc diesel developing 45 bhp. A three-range gearbox gives nine forward and three reverse gears. An engine speed and 540 rpm PTO are fitted.

Fiat Latest in this firm's crawler range are the 90C and 120C powered by 98-bhp four-cylinder and 120-bhp six-cylinder Fiat/OM diesel engines respectively. Both have five forward and one reverse gears. PTO is standard and hydraulic linkage optional.

Folli Super CF 3000 is largest in range and has a Slanzi 36-bhp two-cylinder diesel engine, and six forward and one reverse gears. A 570 rpm PTO is fitted and hydraulic lift is available.

Folli, Italy
Orange with blue engine/transmission and white wheels
Folli produce industrial tractors, fork-lift trucks and small agricultural tractors.

Ford, USA & UK
Blue with white wheels

Henry Ford, being a farmer's son, devoted almost as much attention to mechanizing agriculture as to perfecting his cars before the First World War. He built a prototype tractor in 1907, followed by over fifty others before his famous Model F entered production in 1917. This was one of the earliest mass-produced, unit-built (frameless) machines of a recognizable 'tractor shape' by today's standards. (The first was the Wallis Cub of 1912.)
Many of the first 6000 Ford tractors came to Britain. Ford were making 100,000 tractors a year in the early twenties, and were outselling all the other makers in the USA combined. A small number were produced simultaneously in Ireland, and from 1929 to 1932 this was the only Ford tractor plant. Afterwards production moved to Dagenham, England, where the N model continued to 1945, when it was replaced by the E27N Major. Meanwhile tractor production had restarted at the Ford plant in America in 1939, with the 9N tractor incorporating the Ferguson System, and this was followed by the 8N after the war.
Ford farm tractors are now made in a number of countries, notably the

Fiat First of a range of 'new generation' Fiat-wheeled tractors are the 780/880, and shown here is the 4 × 4 version of the 880. It has a four-cylinder 4562 cc Fiat/OM diesel developing 88 DIN flywheel hp. A two-range gearbox gives eight forward and two reverse gears, and an optional secondary reduction gear gives four forward and two reverse creep speeds. 540 rpm PTO is standard and 1000 rpm PTO available.

Ford The 4100 is a 52-bhp (BS AU 141a) machine, with Ford three-cylinder diesel engine and eight forward and two reverse gears. A similar tractor of 62 bhp is available as the 4600. Power-steering is optional on both.

Ford The 6700 has a four-cylinder 78-bhp (BS AU 141a) Ford diesel engine. Sixteen forward and four reverse gears are provided, and the transmission incorporates Dual Power, which gives a 22 per cent speed reduction and a corresponding 28 per cent more pulling power simply by depressing a pedal.

Ford The 8700 and 9700 share the same 6·6 litre six-cylinder diesel engine, though in the case of the 9700 it is turbocharged and develops 138 DIN hp (153 bhp BS AU 141a). Their Dual Power transmission gives sixteen forward and four reverse gears. Steering is power-assisted and the wheel can be tilted to suit individual drivers.

USA, Britain (320 per day) and Belgium (120 per day). There are some models common to all countries, and engines for most are made in Britain, with European transmissions produced in Belgium. Special variations are produced for particular markets, such as a 4 × 4 for Germany (British 4 × 4s incorporating Ford components are made by Muir-Hill, County and Roadless), vineyard tractors, and a six-cylinder 7100 tractor especially for France. The complete Ford range covers tractors of all sizes from garden models and the 23 PTO hp model 1000 to 138 DIN hp (model 9700).

Ford The 3600 uses a larger stroke version of the three-cylinder Ford diesel engine found in the 2600. It develops 47 bhp (BS AU 141a). A two-range gearbox provides eight forward and two reverse gears. Power-steering is optional. The example shown is in export trim without the safety cab, which is a legal requirement in Britain.

Gévarm, France

The Compagnie des Forges d'Homecourt of St Chamond began to make tracked vehicles over sixty years ago, particularly for military purposes. They were eventually acquired by Gévarm, who have made compact crawler tractors for some thirty years. Their current models are primarily for vineyard work and feature Perkins 47-bhp three-cylinder diesel engines.

Goldoni, Italy
Orange with green engine/transmission

Founded in 1926 to make irrigation pumps, Goldoni made its first motor-cultivator in 1956 and later added 4 × 4 agricultural transporters and small two- and four-wheel drive tractors of up to 36 bhp. In 1975 it was the largest Italian supplier in these categories, with almost 5500 sales in Italy.

Gutbrod, West Germany
Orange with beige wheels

Wilhelm Gutbrod began by making Standard motorcycles in 1926 and in 1930 launched three- and four-wheeled trucks, followed by cars in 1932. In 1939 his firm made a motorized hay-cutter, and in 1952 motor-cultivators followed. The firm now produces Gutbrod/MotoStandard miniature tractors for municipal, garden and nursery use. In 1974 they acquired Bungartz & Peschke, who had produced tractors in Pfalz for over twenty-five years, and now make larger models than the Gutbrod range for vineyard and agricultural use.

Goldoni's two-wheel drive tractors are the two-cylinder 28 DIN hp 828 and the three-cylinder 34 DIN hp 834. The air-cooled Slanzi engined 834 is shown, which has six forward and three reverse gears giving a top speed of 23·7 km/h. Three-point linkage and 550/850 rpm PTO are fitted.

Goldoni make pivot-steering 4 × 4 tractors of 20 to 34 DIN hp. All have air-cooling and six forward and three reverse gears. PTO and hydraulic linkage are standard fitments. The two-cylinder 30 DIN hp 530T model is shown.

Gutbrod make the Bungartz & Peschke narrow-track T 9-DK 50 tractor which can also be equipped with four-wheel drive. It has a three-cylinder 2826 cc Deutz diesel developing 52 DIN hp and eight forward and two reverse gears. Ground speed and 540/1000 rpm PTO are fitted. 30 DIN hp models are also available.

Hagie, USA
Red with white cab and wheels

Originally seed growers, the Hagie family saw the need for special high-clearance tractors and in 1947 formed a company to produce them. They are now the largest manufacturers of high-clearance tractors and these are widely used for crop spraying, sweet-corn cultivation and other rowcrop work.

In addition to the machine shown, Hagie makes a smaller version, the 470 Hi-Tractor, with Ford four-cylinder 68-bhp petrol or Perkins four-cylinder 65-bhp diesel engines, and two- or four-wheel hydrostatic drive, a feature adopted by Hagie tractors in 1968.

Hefty, USA
Yellow with white wheels

Hefty are one of the few companies in America making tractors which fill the gap between the miniature garden and horticultural models (outside the scope of this book), and machines of 60 and more bhp. They make the conventional Model F and the mechanically similar, but rear-engined, Model G for front and mid-mounted rowcrop implements.

Hela, West Germany

A contraction of the maker's name (Hermann Lanz), Hela general-purpose tractors were so named to avoid confusion with Heinrich Lanz of Mannheim, makers of the Lanz Bulldog, who were taken over by John Deere in the 1960s, and who no longer make their own tractors.

Hela have made general-purpose tractors in small numbers since 1929.

Hinomoto, Japan
Red mechanical parts, otherwise yellow

Toyosha is an engineering firm dating back to 1863. It claims to be the largest producer and exporter of compact tractors in Japan (where most production is of under 30-bhp machines). It added Hinomoto tractors to its range of motor-cultivators in the mid-1960s, and makes 10-, 11-, 14- and 22-bhp models with petrol and diesel air-cooled engines of its own or Kawasaki manufacture.

Hefty F has a four-cylinder Continental 27 PTO hp petrol engine, six forward and one reverse gears, hydraulics and 540 rpm PTO.

Hagie 647 Hi-Tractor is powered by 130-bhp eight-cylinder Chrysler petrol engine, or 107-bhp six-cylinder Perkins diesel. Drive is by two- or four-wheel hub-mounted hydrostatic motors which give one-lever control and up to 13 mph. Shown here with 50-foot wide spray boom and two 300-gallon tanks.

Hinomoto MC-220 has a two-cylinder 22-bhp 1055 cc air-cooled diesel engine, and six forward and two reverse gears. A three-speed PTO is fitted and the tractor is normally supplied with mounted cultivator.

Holder, West Germany
Green with red or white wheel. Small 4×2 models are orange

Holder have made crop-sprayers since 1898 and two-wheel horticultural tractors since 1930. They now make two- and four-wheel tractors as well as cultivators, mowers and spraying equipment. Their four-wheel Cultitrac tractors have all-wheel drive and come in 18, 32 and 48 SAE hp sizes.

Hurlimann, Switzerland

A small Swiss maker of general-purpose tractors and machines for mountain farmers.

IMT, Yugoslavia
Red with grey wheels, engine and transmission

Soon after the Second World War Yugoslavia tried twenty-five different tractors to find the one most suited to local requirements. The Ferguson was selected and this was built under licence until 1968, when the agreement expired. Subsequent IMT tractors have generally been loosely based on their former Fergusons and in many cases still use Perkins engines. The current range covers tractors of 33 to 220 bhp.

Holder A55 Cultitrac 4 × 4 tractor has pivot-steering, a three-cylinder Holder 2·02-litre diesel developing 48 SAE hp, and eight forward and four reverse gears. A 540 rpm PTO is fitted and the three-point linkage has a lifting capacity of 1597 kg. The machine is also used for municipal snow clearance and timber extraction.

IMT 540 has three-cylinder 2½-litre diesel developing 39 PTO hp, and six forward and two reverse gears.

IMT 5200 all-wheel drive tractor can have Famos 220-bhp six-cylinder or Mercedes V-8 207-bhp diesels. It has pivot-steering and eight forward and one reverse gears.

International, UK & USA
Red and white

The merger of a number of implement-makers including the McCormick and Deering firms in 1902 resulted in the International Harvester Co., which began to make tractors three years later. Their famous Titan and Mogul ranges appeared in 1910, and versions of these were used in their thousands in Britain during the First World War. In the early 1920s these were replaced by the general-purpose Farmall (one of the first tractors with PTO, as opposed to simply a belt pulley) and by the 10/20 and 15/30, the smaller of which remained little changed for almost twenty years.

A new Farmall range appeared in 1939 alongside the larger Internationals, and in 1949 IHC began its world-wide expansion by setting up a British factory. Here Anglicized versions of their tractors were joined by the first wholly British International, the B-250, in 1956. International tractors and other farm equipment is currently made in the USA and a number of overseas countries, and include 50- and 60-bhp crawlers, as well as 4 × 2 models up to 160 bhp and 4 × 4 models up to 178 bhp. 4 × 4 machines of higher horsepowers are produced by Steiger, in whom IHC hold a financial interest, and some are sold (e.g. in Australia) in IHC colours.

International Smallest of the British-built range is the 374. It has a four-cylinder 35 DIN hp (30 PTO hp) diesel and eight forward and two reverse gears.

International This unique machine is the 574 Hydro. It has hydrostatic infinitely variable transmission, and hydraulics and PTO working entirely independently of engine/ground speed. The standard 574 has a four-cylinder 66 DIN hp (54 PTO hp) diesel. It is also available with four-wheel drive and eight forward and four reverse gears, or double that quantity with torque amplifier. A larger 104 PTO hp Hydro model is produced in the USA.

International The German-built 1046 can have two- or four-wheel drive and has twelve forward and five reverse gears, with full synchromesh. Its six-cylinder diesel develops 100 DIN hp (92 PTO hp).

International's largest kingpin, as opposed to pivot-steer, 4 × 4 model is the 4166. It has a 178 bhp six-cylinder turbocharged International diesel engine, and eight forward and four reverse gears. Two- or four-wheel steering can be selected by the driver.

International Largest of the American range of two-wheel drive International tractors is the 1586 with six-cylinder 436 cu. in. turbocharged diesel engine of 160 PTO hp (140 drawbar hp). It has six forward and three reverse gears, or double that number of ratios with torque amplifier.

Iseki, Japan
Royal blue with white wheels, and black engine and transmission

Iseki make various two- and four-wheel drive tractors of 13 to 35 bhp. The largest models have many interchangeable parts and two- and three-cylinder Isuzu water-cooled diesel engines.

Kharkov, USSR
Pale blue and pale yellow with white wheels

This Soviet tractor factory makes various wheeled and crawler tractors using 165-bhp diesel engines and as many other common parts as possible. There is 70 per cent parts interchangeability between the T-150 crawler and T-150K shown.

Kirov, USSR
Orange with white cab and wheels

The first Soviet tractor was built in this factory in 1924 and since the mid-1960s this maker has specialized in high horsepower 4×4 machines. The current K-701 was introduced in 1975 and is one of the largest wheeled agricultural tractors currently produced.

Kharkov T-150K four-wheel drive tractor has 165-bhp diesel and two-speed hydraulically driven PTO, plus implement lift.

Iseki TS3510 has a three-cylinder Isuzu diesel of 1777 cc capacity and 35 bhp output. It has eight forward and two reverse gears, three-point linkage and four-speed PTO.

Kirov The K-701 has a V-12 diesel of 300 DIN hp and a mechanical/hydraulic four-range gearbox giving sixteen forward and four reverse gears. It has pivot-steering, can tow sixty tonnes and has conventional three-point hydraulic linkage.

Komatsu, Japan
Yellow

Komatsu started by making mining machinery in 1921 and in 1932 introduced crawler tractors. This firm now makes dump trucks and crawler tractors for construction and quarrying, and some of the smaller tractors (35 to 180 bhp) are available for agricultural use. Many Komatsu vehicles use American Cummins engines made under licence in Japan.

Kramer, West Germany
Yellow with red wheels

Since its foundation in 1937 Kramer has made special-purpose tractors for road haulage, forestry and agriculture. It now makes four-wheel drive tractors for various industrial purposes with air-cooled Deutz engines of 32 to 121 DIN hp. Some of these are available for agricultural use, notably the Zweiwege-trac (Two-way-trac) 1014. Kramer front-drive axles are used on some Case/David Brown 4 × 4 models.

Kubota, Japan
Orange with blue mechanical parts

Kubota made their first tractor in 1960 and now produce diesel engines, construction machinery, cultivators, small combine harvesters, paddy-field machinery and four-wheeled tractors of 12·5, 17, 20, 24 and 26 bhp. These tractors can have two- or four-wheel drive, and all are fitted with Kubota water-cooled diesel engines.

Kramer The 1014 has four-wheel drive, four-wheel steering and sixteen gears in either direction. It has a six-cylinder 5652 cc air-cooled diesel engine developing 105, 112 or 121 bhp.

Komatsu D50A has a 90-bhp four-cylinder 7240 cc diesel engine and weighs 9·5 tonnes. It has four forward and three reverse gears.

Kubota L245DT has a 26-bhp water-cooled three-cylinder diesel engine of 1115 cc capacity, and has eight forward and two reverse gears, with double that number optionally available. A three-speed PTO is fitted and the tractor has four-wheel drive.

Labourier, France

Labourier is a small French manufacturer of agricultural transporters and mountain and general-purpose tractors. These are assembled from various bought-in parts, and Georges Irat, Steyr and Perkins diesel engines have been used.

Lamborghini, Italy
Blue and white

Soon after the Second World War Ferruccio Lamborghini began to make agricultural equipment from war surplus machinery. By 1949 he was producing tractors and tuning cars as a hobby. This hobby led to the high-performance Lamborghini cars introduced in 1963. In 1972 the car and tractor sides of the company separated, the latter being bought by SAME. Today Lamborghini build approximately 5000 tractors per year, and offer crawlers and wheeled models of up to 115 SAE hp—the latter with four-wheel drive.

Lamborghini 854 is available with two- or four-wheel drive (R or DT prefix). It has a 4160 cc four-cylinder air-cooled diesel of 82 DIN hp, and twelve forward and four reverse gears giving up to 24 km/h, plus an optional four forward and one reverse creeper range. 540 and 1000 rpm PTO is standard.

Lamborghini make 38, 59 and 69 SAE hp crawlers, of which the middle C553 model is shown here with wide and narrow tracks. It has a three-cylinder 165·7 cu. in. Lamborghini diesel engine, and eight forward and four reverse gears giving up to 11 km/h. 540 rpm PTO and three-point linkage are fitted.

Landini, Italy
Blue with grey wheels and engine/transmission

Landini grew from a blacksmith's business founded in 1884, and in 1925 it produced its first tractor. It was the largest Italian producer for many years, specializing in semi-diesel machines until, in 1957, the firm obtained a licence to make and install Perkins's diesels. In 1959 Massey-Ferguson acquired the British Perkins company, and in the following year they bought Landini as well. Since that time Landini tractors have retained their individuality and the company now produces 53, 67, 75, 84 and 95 SAE hp two- and four-wheel drive machines, and various medium-weight crawlers, some of which are sold in Massey-Ferguson colours in place of Landini's blue. They also supply front-wheel drive axles to overseas Massey-Ferguson factories.

Landini The smallest is the 5500 available with two-, or as shown here, four-wheel drive. It is powered by the Perkins P3 three-cylinder 53 SAE hp diesel, and has twelve forward and four reverse gears giving up to 15·63 mph forwards. Four-wheel drive can be disengaged and the front axle has epicyclic reduction gears in the wheel hubs. The specification includes a choice of PTOs as well as hydraulic lift with draft control, disc brakes and differential lock.

Leyland, UK
Blue with silver grey stripe and wheels

The predecessor of the Leyland tractor was the Nuffield introduced in 1948 by Lord Nuffield, the founder of Morris Motors. In 1953 Austin and Morris merged to form BMC, who added a second ratio to the Nuffield's original five forward speed gearbox in 1963. BMC joined with the well-known commercial vehicle makers, Leyland in 1968, and in the following year the tractor models became known as Leylands, and their orange colour scheme was changed to the present light blue.

Leyland's Scottish factory now produces wheeled tractors of 25 to 100 hp; the company also owns the makers of the Aveling-Marshall crawler. 4 × 4 versions of Leyland tractors with equal-sized wheels are produced by Bray Construction Machinery Ltd.

Landini 6500 crawler is powered by a Perkins 65-bhp four-cylinder diesel and has eight forward and four reverse gears giving up to 24 km/h. Independent and engine speed PTOs are fitted and hydraulic lift and draft control as on Landini wheeled tractors can be specified.

Leyland The 2100 and the similar 285 both have Leyland six-cylinder diesel engines, of 100 and 85 bhp respectively (81 and 67 hp at the slowest of the two standard speeds of the independent PTO). Ten forward and two reverse gears are provided and four-wheel drive versions with equal-sized wheels all round; the 485 and 4100, are also available.

LIAZ, Czechoslovakia

LIAZ has been producing heavy vehicles for some 25 years and is responsible for the Skoda truck programme. It has recently introduced a large 4 × 4, king-pin steer, agricultural tractor using a Skoda diesel engine.

Long, USA
Blue with white wheels

Though sold in their own livery and bearing the Long name, these 32 to 104 PTO horsepower tractors are in fact imported from various European manufacturers, notably Zetor and Universal.

Mailam, Italy

Mailam make industrial and agricultural crawler tractors based on British Ford mechanical units.

Mailam 5001 has a Ford 3846 cc four-cylinder diesel engine developing 67 bhp. It has seven forward and two reverse gears, 540 rpm PTO and a top speed of 11 km/h.

LIAZ 4 × 4 tractor has transverse leaf spring and pivot front suspension, two range, five speed Praga gearbox and 11·94 litre, six cylinder, 192 bhp Skoda diesel engine.

Malves MD 920P has a six-cylinder Mercedes-Benz 5·675-litre diesel developing 120 SAE hp. There is a two-range transmission giving ten forward and two reverse speeds, with a maximum of 30 km/h. A four-wheel drive version is also available.

Malves, Brazil
Yellow

One of the few indigenous tractor-makers in Brazil is Malves, who produce Mercedes-Benz and Cummins engined crawlers, primarily for the construction industry, and 70 and 120 SAE hp wheeled agricultural tractors.

Massey-Ferguson, Canada & UK
Red and silver grey

The amalgamation of the Canadian Massey-Harris and British Ferguson firms in 1953 led to the development of joint Massey-Ferguson tractors, produced from 1957, and the adoption of the familiar red and grey colour scheme from 1958.

Massey-Harris history goes back to Daniel Massey's original machine shop of 1847 and the 1891 merger with agricultural machinery rivals, the Harris Co (founded 1857). Some steam tractors were sold in their early years and later the firm supplied various American makes of internal combustion-engined tractor in Canada. In 1927 they purchased the makers of the Wallis tractor and in 1930 introduced their own first design, one of the earliest four-wheel drive tractors to be commercially successful.

Meanwhile Harry Ferguson of Ulster had sold a number of ploughs in Ireland and America. He was dissatisfied with the way that tractors had been developed as simple replacements for draught animals and wanted a more sophisticated machine, to which implements could be directly mounted. After years of experiment he built a prototype tractor in 1933 which could be said

Massey-Ferguson
This North American MF 230 is powered by a Perkins three-cylinder diesel developing 34 PTO horsepower, or by a four-cylinder Continental petrol engine of similar output. Six forward and two reverse gears give up to 14·5 mph. The three-point linkage can lift up to 2075 lb and a 'live' PTO is standard.

Massey-Ferguson A British-built MF 590. The 500 Series introduced in Britain in May 1976 covers (DIN Ratings) 47 hp MF 550, 60 hp MF 565, 66 hp MF 575, 88 hp MF 595 and the 75 hp MF 590 shown here. All have Perkins diesel engines and choice of dual range, eight forward/two reverse gears, or twelve speed plus four reverse change-on-the-move Multi-Power transmission.

Massey-Ferguson
This British-built MF1200 has pivot-steering and a 25-foot turning circle. Power comes from a 110-bhp Perkins six-cylinder diesel engine of 5801 cc capacity. It has Multi-Power twelve forward and four reverse gear transmission with four-wheel drive, Ferguson System hydraulics and 1000 rpm PTO.

to be the forerunner of virtually all modern tractors and, following successful trials, David Brown made the first production versions in 1936. They incorporated hydraulic implement lifts and draft control, which kept implements working at a pre-determined depth whatever the angle of the tractor. The geometry of the three-point linkage put the weight transference from the mounted implement forward of the tractors back axle for optimum traction and stability. In 1939 Ford started to build tractors incorporating the Ferguson System in America and from 1946 Ferguson tractors were built in Britain by the Standard Motor Co.

Following the amalgamation of Harry Ferguson's interests with Massey-Harris in 1953, Massey-Ferguson became the world's largest producer of tractors and now has over forty factories world-wide, notably in Canada, Britain, USA, Germany, France, Argentina, Brazil and Italy. It controls a number of other tractor firms including Landini (whose crawlers it markets outside Italy as MFs). In 1959 Frank Perkins Ltd of Peterborough, England, the largest producer of diesel engines in the world was acquired and now many Massey-Ferguson tractors have Perkins Engines.

As some MF tractor models are produced with minor variations in all the major factories, while others are specifically for local requirements, it is possible to illustrate only a representative selection of them here.

Massey-Ferguson
The MF 1155 is one of the largest two-wheel drive tractors available in Britain and has a Perkins V-8 diesel of 155 DIN hp (140 PTO hp). It has Multi-Power eight forward/four reverse transmission and two speed PTO. Hydraulic implement lift capacity is 6938 lb.

Massey-Ferguson
The largest North American two-wheel drive Massey-Ferguson is the 190 PTO hp MF 2800 with turbocharged Perkins V-8 diesel engine and eight speed manual or twenty-four speed (option of three gears within each of eight gears) Multi-Speed transmission.

Massey-Ferguson Various 4 × 4 models are available and the largest American-built models are the MF 1505 and 1805. Both have similar 636 cu. in. Caterpillar V-8 diesels of 185 SAE hp (174 PTO hp) and 210 SAE hp (192 PTO hp) respectively, twelve forward and four reverse gears giving up to 20·81 mph, and centre pivot-steering. Three-point hitch and PTO are optional.

Mercedes-Benz, West Germany
White with red wheels, wings and steps. Unimogs usually green

Mercedes-Benz dates from 1926, when two pioneer motor manufacturers, Daimler and Benz, joined forces. In 1922 Benz had produced the world's first diesel agricultural tractor and for many years both Mercedes origin single-cylinder and Benz origin multi-cylinder tractors were produced. In the 1950s the company re-entered the agricultural field with their multi-purpose Unimog four-wheel drive tractors and load-carriers, which are now made in a variety of sizes from 34 to 120 DIN hp. More recently they developed a wholly agricultural MB Trac range.

Mercedes-Benz The MB Trac 800 has a four-cylinder 3780 cc 72 DIN hp diesel engine and up to 24 forward gears. Live front and rear-mounted 540/1000 rpm PTO is fitted, and there are differential locks on both axles. The example shown has front and rear three-point linkage, with draft control on the latter. MB Tracs of 65–125 DIN hp are available.

Mercedes-Benz Unimogs come in a variety of sizes and only some are specifically intended for agriculture, when three-point linkage and PTO are usually fitted. Shown is a model 406 (AG) with 84 DIN hp six-cylinder diesel and twelve forward and four reverse gears, plus eight forward and four reverse crawler gears.

Minneapolis-Moline, USA
White

Minneapolis-Moline joined the White empire in 1963 and their name has now been almost entirely replaced on tractors by that of White. The firm dates from 1929, when the makers of the Twin City, Minneapolis, and former Moline tractors merged. The combined firm produced a wide range of machines including some of the first with enclosed cabs in 1938, and supplied many tractors to Britain during the Second World War. In more recent years M-M (as they are often abbreviated) have specialized in large, powerful tractors for the vast fields of the USA grain belt.

Mitsubishi, Japan
Grey mechanical parts, silver grille, red wheels, wings and engine cover

Mitsubishi, which means Three Diamonds in Japanese, began over a hundred years ago in the shipping and heavy engineering business. They assembled their first car in 1917, followed by commercial vehicles from 1932. Since 1971 Chrysler has had a financial stake in Mitsubishi Motors, which became an independent company in 1970. In the agricultural field Mitsubishi makes 15- to 45-bhp wheeled tractors, and also produces Caterpillar machines under licence (primarily for the Japanese construction industry).

Minneapolis-Moline
The G955 was first introduced in 1973 and is one of the last tractors to bear the M-M name, though it was sold in Canada from the outset as the White 1870. It has an M-M 97 PTO hp six-cylinder diesel (a 92 PTO hp engine running on LPG was also available) and its transmission was originally designed by M-M's associates, Oliver.

Mitsubishi R 3500G has a four-cylinder, 2084 cc 35-bhp diesel engine, ten forward and two reverse gears and 540, 740, 1060 and 1420 rpm PTO.

MRS A-100 has a six cylinder, nine litre (552 cu in) GM Detroit two-stroke diesel developing 322 bhp and ten forward and two reverse gears. It is shown with optional farm dozer blade and has 48,300 lbs drawbar pull and a top speed of 20 mph.

MRS, USA
Yellow

Founded in 1943, and one of the pioneers of big horsepower 4 × 4 tractors in the late 1950s, MRS has been better known for vehicles for the construction industry in the intervening years. However, it is now taking a renewed interest in agricultural tractors and makes Detroit diesel-engined 167–322 bhp machines, with 10/2 forward/reverse gears respectively. They have four-wheel kingpin as opposed to pivot-steering, both axles having independent or co-ordinated steering.

Muir-Hill, UK
Yellow with white cab

Muir-Hill were pioneers of converting Fordson agricultural tractors for industrial and earth-moving purposes. Their first conversion was in 1927 for heavy towing on the road, and they later made crawler tractors, as well as a successful line of Ford-based dumpers.

In 1966 they introduced one of the first big 4 × 4 tractors in Britain, the 101 (now the 120 bhp 121 model) with Ford six-cylinder diesel. It was joined by the Perkins-engined 110 (now 110 bhp 111 model) and by the Perkins V-8 engined 171. Muir-Hill tractors are now in use in some fifty countries.

Nibbi, Italy

Nibbi make both two- and four-wheel drive models ranging from 14·5 to 29 bhp. The 4 × 4 types have equal-sized wheels and pivot-steering.

Nibbi RM2/20S has a two-cylinder Slanzi air-cooled diesel engine of 1330 cc capacity and 29 bhp output. It has six forward and one reverse gears, giving up to 17 km/h. Ground speed and 600 rpm PTO are provided and hydraulic lift is available.

Muir-Hill Most powerful tractor in the range is the 177-bhp Perkins V-8 engined 171. It has a ten forward and two reverse speed constant mesh gearbox and a top speed of 21·6 mph. Weight distribution on the double reduction planetary axles is $66\frac{2}{3}$ per cent front and $33\frac{1}{3}$ on rear when unladen, to provide equal loading when drawing an implement. A hydrostatic 1000 rpm PTO of 120 bhp is provided, plus three-point linkage.

Oliver, USA
Green and white

Oliver has been owned by White Motor Corp since 1960 and its name is being replaced gradually by that of White. James Oliver began making ploughs in 1855, and in 1929 the company that he had founded merged with Hart-Parr, who had produced tractors on a commercial basis since 1902. The resulting Oliver-Hart-Parr name continued on tractors until the late thirties, and afterwards they became simply Olivers with advanced streamline styling. The makers of the Cletrac joined the firm in 1944 and crawlers were produced until 1965. From 1960 to 1963 David Brown supplied tractors to Oliver to augment the lighter end of their range, and since 1967 a similar arrangement has existed with Fiat, whose tractors are now sold in North America as Whites.

PGS, Italy

PGS make typical Italian 4×4 pivot-steer tractors for small farms and vineyards. They use Slanzi, Lombardini and Ruggerini air-cooled diesels of 18 to 30 bhp.

Pinza, Italy
Pale green with orange wheels

Pinza have made motor-cultivators for over twenty years. These, together with pumps and small 4×4 agricultural load-carriers, account for most of their current production, but they have recently introduced a 4×4 pivot-steer tractor of the typical Italian type for vineyards and small farms.

PGS The Roma 30-13 has a 28-bhp two-cylinder Slanzi diesel engine, six forward and two reverse gears, ground speed and 670 rpm PTO, optional hydraulic lift and a 24 km/h top speed.

Oliver White-Oliver 1955 has a six-cylinder turbocharged 108-bhp diesel, hydraulically powered PTO, and choice of twelve- or eighteen-speed transmission. 4×4 versions have also been produced.

Pinza Grillo 4×4 pivot-steer tractor has a two-cylinder 30-bhp diesel engine, six forward and two reverse gears and 1000 rpm PTO.

Ranger, Italy

Isotta Fraschini made cars from 1900 and in their early years were second only to Fiat in size. In the 1920s and '30s they made luxury cars as well as commercial vehicles and aero-engines. After the Second World War they were bought by rival aero-engine maker Breda, and now concentrate on small 4 × 4 Ranger tractors and general engineering.

Reform, Austria
Red with white wheels and cab roof

Founded in 1910, the company concentrated on agricultural implements, particularly seed-drills, which it still makes today. After the Second World War it began to make motorized forage harvesters for upland pastures, and in 1968 it introduced the Reform Muli, a 4 × 4 tool- and load-carrier able to work on 60 per cent slopes. In 1977 the company introduced the Reform Metrac 3000 as a tractor and general implement carrier for hill farms.

Ranger PD 150/4R has a single-cylinder Lombardini 638 cc air-cooled diesel engine developing 15 bhp. It has six forward and two reverse gears, pivot-steering, three-speed PTO and three-point linkage.

Renault, France
Orange with white wheels

Renault have made vehicles since 1902 and following experience with tracked *char d'assaût* in the First World War, they introduced agricultural crawlers in 1919. These in turn led to wheeled tractors in the mid-twenties. Renault now make twenty-five distinct models from small 30 DIN hp vineyard models up to the largest 145 DIN hp 1451−4 tractor. MWM engines from Mannheim are used right across the range and, following the sale of Carraro tractors in France as Renault-Carraros, the Italian company now supplies all-wheel drive components to Renault's own 4 × 4 tractors.

Reform Metrac 3000 has a two-cylinder 35-bhp (DIN) diesel engine, eight forward and eight reverse gears, four-wheel drive and rear-wheel steering. It is shown here with a front-mounted cutter bar and trailed tedder.

Renault Largest in the range is the 1451-4 model with 145 DIN hp (160 SAE hp) MWM 6234 cc six-cylinder diesel engine. It has three-range transmission giving a total of fifteen forward and six reverse gears. 1000 rpm PTO and three-point linkage are standard.

Assembly takes place at a new factory at Le Mans, where approximately 16,000 tractors are produced each year, of which roughly 3500 are exported.

The State-owned Renault company also controls the Saviem commercial firm formed in 1955 by the merger of Latil and Somua. Latil have made four-wheel drive and four-wheel steer tractors since before the First World War, primarily for heavy haulage, military and forestry purposes. Many have, however, been used in agriculture and, in 1927, were the first tractors in the world (albeit not solely for farming purposes) with pneumatic tyres. Some are still used in France for winch ploughing.

Roadless, UK
Blue and white

Roadless started in the early 1920s making half-track conversions to enable commercial vehicles to work off the road. This experience was applied to agricultural vehicles soon afterwards and from 1936 the company concentrated on full and half-track tractors. In more recent years they have switched their attention to all-wheel drive machines based on Ford components, and now make machines ranging from the 78-bhp Ploughmaster 78 to the Roadless 118, all with unequal-sized front and rear wheels, plus the Roadless 120 with equal-sized wheels all round.

Renault 951 has a six-cylinder MWM 95 DIN hp (104 SAE hp) 5656 cc diesel engine. A three-range gearbox gives twelve forward and twelve reverse gears, and an extra range to give sixteen gears in each direction is available. 540/1000 rpm PTO is standard as well as three-point linkage. A 4 × 4 version is also offered.

Renault have a large selection of small general-purpose and vineyard models. The six to the left have air-cooled MWM two- and three-cylinder diesel engines of 30 to 51 DIN hp, while the two to the right have water-cooled (like their larger sisters) MWM three and four-cylinder diesel engines of 55 (model 556) and 65 (model 656) DIN hp. Standard versions of the models to the left with similar styling to those on the right are also produced.

SAME A 78 DIN hp four-cylinder 4156 cc Saturno 4 × 4 showing its low profile and consequent low centre of gravity. It has eight forward and four reverse gears, with optional extra reduction, and a top speed of 30 km/h.

Roadless 118 has a Ford six-cylinder 114 bhp (BS one-hour rating) and sixteen speed Ford Dual Power Transmission giving up to 19·2 mph. The front axle has planetary drive to reduce torque-loading on the axle shafts and on the differential, which is lockable.

SAME, Italy
Red with blue wheel centres and mechanical parts

One of the first true diesel tractors, the 40 bhp two-cylinder Cassani, was developed in 1927 by Francesco Cassani, who went on to found SAME. Production of SAME tractors commenced in 1948, when 33 left the works, and by 1971 there were more SAMEs than any other type of 4 × 4 tractor in Italy. The range covers eleven horsepower sizes from the 30 DIN hp Sirenetta to the 126 DIN hp Buffalo, and all have air-cooling and were initially designed with four-wheel drive, although about 30 per cent of the 20,000 SAME tractors produced each year are 4 × 2 machines. SAME also owns the Lamborghini tractor firm.

SAME The Buffalo 130 has a 126 DIN hp 6234 cc six-cylinder air-cooled diesel, and twelve forward and four reverse gears, with the option of double that number. It has two-speed independent PTO.

Satoh, Japan
Red and white

Satoh make various small tractors including the Beaver 15-bhp, Elk 19.5-bhp, Bison 27-bhp and Stallion 38-bhp machines.

Schilter, Switzerland
Red and white

Schilter make a variety of four-wheel drive transporters and tool-carriers for hill farmers. They use MWM, Perkins, Lombardini or MAG engines. A recent introduction has been the general-purpose UT (Universal Tractor) with four-wheel drive/four-wheel steering.

Satoh The Stallion has a three-cylinder 1777 cc water-cooled 38-bhp diesel engine, and nine forward and three reverse gears giving up to 26 km/h. 540/1000 rpm PTO is fitted as well as hydraulic linkage, and a twelve forward speed gearbox is available.

Schilter UT 5000 has 65-bhp four-cylinder Perkins diesel and two range, eight forward and four reverse speed gearbox. Front and rear PTO and three-point linkage are provided, and rear wheel steering can be locked out for certain mounted implements.

Schlüter Super 9500 TVL has a 200-bhp diesel engine, automatic differential locks and Schlüter-Hydromatik transmission. It is shown here with a semi-mounted eight-furrow plough.

Schlüter, West Germany
Red and grey with cream wheels

Founded in 1905 to make portable engines for powering agricultural and other machinery, Schlüter concentrated on diesel engines of 5 to 240 hp from 1930, and in 1937, they introduced their first tractor—the 14 hp DZM cold-starting diesel model. During the war they made several tractors with producer-gas engines and afterwards concentrated on 25 hp two-cylinder diesels. In the later forties they developed single-cylinder 15 hp diesel tractors and multi-cylinder models of up to 60 hp. Thereafter they specialized in big horsepower machines and now make 85- and 100-bhp tractors with two- or four-wheel drive, and 18-speed synchromesh gearboxes, and 4 × 4 models of 100 to 350 bhp, as well as an extensive range of diesel engines.

Steiger, USA
Light yellow green with red wheels

Founded in the late 1960s, Steiger has become one of the world's major producers of large 4 × 4 tractors, with current sales of over 100 million dollars per year. In 1975 International Harvester bought a 39 per cent stake in the company, and today Steiger make some of the largest International models. Steiger also made Allis-Chalmers' big 4 × 4 models before A-C developed its own range. At the moment of going to press, Steiger are reported to be working on a range of giant tractors for Ford. The Steiger range covers 210- to 650-bhp pivot-steer models, the latter comprising two tractors with their rear-axle units removed and the motor-unit joined together at a central pivot. Steiger use Caterpillar and Cummins diesel engines.

Steiger Apart from the 650-bhp Twin-Panther, the Steiger Panther model line includes the Caterpillar six-cylinder engined ST-325, the Cummins V-8 engined ST-320 and the Cummins six-cylinder ST-310 shown here. In each case the model numbers signify bhp. The ST-310 has ten forward and two reverse gears and stereo radio/tape deck plus air-conditioning as standard features.

Schlüter Among the most powerful European wheeled tractors is the 350-bhp Profi Trac 3500 TVL which has four-wheel drive and four-wheel steering. It is often fitted with twin 20·8 × 38 AS tyres all round.

Steyr, Austria
Red and white with grey mechanical parts

The famous Austrian armaments firm of Steyr began to make bicycles in 1894 and added cars in 1920. In 1934 it merged with Austro-Daimler, which had manufactured many types of motor vehicle, originally under licence from Daimler in Germany. Austro-Daimler had itself joined forces with the bicycle and motor-vehicle-making firm of Puch in 1928. In 1947 farm tractors were added to Steyr-Daimler-Puch's existing range, and in the next eighteen years more than 160,000 were made, primarily small 15- to 18-bhp single-cylinder machines. Larger horsepower tractors were developed in the fifties and by the mid-sixties went up to 68 bhp. Today the range covers two- and four-wheel drive tractors of up to 140 DIN hp, as well as the multi-purpose Haflinger cross-country vehicle.

Steyr The 1400a (known as 8160a when exported) has a six-cylinder 155-bhp (140 DIN, 125 PTO hp) 6·592-litre diesel engine, and up to thirty-six forward and twelve reverse gears (twelve forward and four reverse gears are standard). Top speed is 20 mph and maximum drawbar lift 10,782 lb. A 1200 rpm PTO is fitted.

Steyr The 760 (760a when 4 × 4) has a four-cylinder 3140 cc 66-bhp diesel engine and four forward gears in each of four ranges, with eight reverse gears. 540/1000 rpm PTO is standard and a cab is available.

Steyr 1200a is a 4 × 4 tractor with six-cylinder 125-bhp diesel engine, and twelve forward and six reverse gears. Hydraulic lift capacity is 8380 lb and the two-wheel drive 1200 of similar specification is available.

Tecnoma, France
Blue and white

Since 1955 Ets Derot Père et Fils of Saacy-sur-Marne have specialized in tractors for vineyard cultivation and these are now distributed by Tecnoma. A special feature of Derot tractors is their ability to straddle vines and other rowcrops such as maize, cotton, pineapples and tea bushes. They come in a variety of sizes giving up to 1·71 metres centre clearance, and offer a choice of 44 SAE hp Renault petrol, MWM 40 SAE hp diesel, or Lombardini 40, 46 or 58 SAE hp diesel engines.

Thomas, UK
Blue and white

Thomas are agricultural contractors and machinery exporters who required a moderately-priced 100-bhp tractor for forage harvesting and general-purpose work. In 1971 they built their first Ninety Five—100 tractor, using the suitably modified rear end of a secondhand four-cylinder Ford 5000 with a new load-bearing frame at the front to accommodate a Ford six-cylinder industrial diesel unit. Since then over a hundred similar machines have been made and several exported to the Republic of Ireland, USA and other countries.

Universal, Romania
Orange with blue mechanical parts and white cab roof

Universal tractors have been made since 1947, are based on Fiat designs, and now include both wheel and crawler models, the former with two- or four-wheel drive. The engine and many other components are common throughout the 445 range, and fuel pump and certain electrical equipment is of British origin. In the USA certain Universal models are sold under the name Long, in blue livery.

Thomas The Ninety Five—100 has the eight-speed transmission of a Ford 5000, and either a 380 or 360 cu. in. six-cylinder Ford diesel engine giving up to 115 bhp (90 PTO hp). A pressurized cab to exclude dust is normally fitted and power-steering is standard.

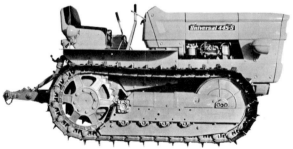

Universal 445-S crawler has three-cylinder 45 DIN hp diesel, and six forward and two reverse gears. A 540 rpm PTO and three-point linkage are fitted as standard.

Tecnoma/Derot tractor demonstrates its ability to straddle a row of vines and hoe on both sides of them at the same time.

Universal 445 and 550 models are outwardly similar except that the smallest shares the three-cylinder diesel with the 445-S crawler, while the 550 has a four-cylinder 55 DIN hp engine. They have 9/3 and 8/2 gears respectively, though when supplied with 4 × 4 the 550 has 12/3 gears. Ground speed and 540 rpm PTO are fitted.

Ursus, Poland
Orange with pale blue frame and mechanical parts and cream wheels

Ursus have made tractors for some twenty-five years based on Zetor designs and now produce four- and six-cylinder models including 85 and 120 SAE hp machines with two- or four-wheel drive.

Valmet, Finland
Light brown with mustard yellow bonnet sides, wheels and cab. White wheels on 1502

Valmet is a large Finnish engineering and shipbuilding group which, in 1953, added tractors to existing small arms production at its Tourula works. The first were 13 hp machines, and from 1955 the models grew in horsepower size to today's brown and mustard-coloured 54 to 150 hp range. Valmet were early in offering synchromesh gearboxes with their 565 tractor in 1965, and have been fitting cabs as standard equipment for over ten years; they supplied their first Q-cab equipped tractor as long ago as 1971. In 1975 they introduced the unique 1502 six-wheel model, which is claimed to reduce soil compaction, reduce the swinging effect of mounted implements, and to improve operator comfort and speed.

Valmet make 3500 tractors per year in Finland and 17,000 at their Brazilian subsidiary. This was established in 1960 and makes a range tailored to South American requirements, where its sales are second only to Massey-Ferguson.

Valmet 502 has 54 SAE hp three-cylinder diesel, and six forward and two reverse gears, plus optional creeper gear. A 540 rpm PTO is fitted plus an 1100 rpm belt pulley.

Ursus The 1201 has a six-cylinder 6839 cc 112 DIN 120 SAE hp diesel engine. It has eight forward and four reverse gears, with double that number if the optional 1:1·34 'torque amplifier' is fitted. A 540/1000 rpm PTO is fitted.

Valmet The 1102 is available with two- or four-wheel drive, and is one of the largest diesel tractors with a four-cylinder engine. This is supercharged and develops 115 SAE hp. It can have eight forward and two reverse gears, or an extra range doubling these ratios.

Valpadana The Super Padano 4RM-L30 has a two-cylinder 1346 cc air-cooled Lombardini diesel engine developing 30 bhp. Four forward and one reverse gears give up to 18 km/h. 540 and 1000 rpm PTO is standard, as is three-point hydraulic linkage.

Valmet The 1502 has an all-wheel drive rear bogie with a central axle taking drive to the wheels via pivoting gearcases (as on Scammell off-road lorries since 1927). Tracks can be fitted over the rear wheels in twenty minutes, and the rear wheels can be lifted for tight turns. Power comes from Valmet six-cylinder supercharged 150 SAE hp diesel, and there are sixteen forward and four reverse gears.

Vladimir T25 has a two-cylinder air-cooled diesel of 28 PTO hp and eight forward gears. The six highest of these are duplicated in reverse, and the seat and controls are reversible so that the tractor can work with equal facility in either direction.

Valpadana, Italy

Valpadana makes 14–30 bhp 4 × 4 pivot-steering tractors for the smaller Italian farms and vineyards. They are also assembled in Spain by Ebro.

Venieri, Italy

A small Italian maker of vineyard tractors using single- and twin-cylinder air-cooled diesel engines.

Versa, USA

Larson make special high-clearance rowcrop tractors with Ford 70-bhp diesel, or Volkswagen 53-bhp petrol engines. They are 4 × 2 machines, but the smaller model can be fitted with an extra set of wheels and half-tracks for difficult conditions.

Versatile, Canada

Versatile concentrates on large 4 × 4 pivot-steering tractors with Cummins diesel engines. Most are in the 200- to 300-bhp category, and have twelve forward and four reverse gears.

Vladimir, USSR
Red with white wheels

Tractors have been made at the Vladimir works since 1944. From 1959, their speciality has been air-cooled diesel engines for farm implements and for the Lipetsk tractor, as well as for their own T25 machine, of which some 7000 are exported each year. 2500 T25 tractors are assembled in Mexico each year as the Sidena T25 model (when they are painted orange).

Volgograd, USSR
Orange with white or pale blue cab roof

Volgograd made their first tractor in 1930 and their millionth in 1975. Annual production is now 80,000 crawlers per year, of which some 5000 are exported. Other larger horsepower Russian crawlers are made by the Cheliabinsk, Onezhiski and Bryansk works, but are primarily for use outside agriculture.

Volvo BM, Sweden
Red with green engine

The origins of Bolinder-Munktell go back to 1832 when J T Munktell founded an agricultural and general engineering business. In 1848 it made Sweden's first locomotive, and in 1913 its first agricultural tractor. Engines were bought from Bolinders and the two companies merged in 1950 and were bought by Volvo, who had made cars and trucks since 1927. In the next twenty-five years some 230,000 Volvo BM tractors were produced and the company now has a joint component development programme with International Harvester and makes 44- to 147-bhp tractors, some with four-wheel drive.

Vladimir The Lipetsk T40A Super uses an air-cooled 53 PTO hp four-cylinder Vladimir diesel based on the two-cylinder unit in the T25. It has eleven forward and two reverse gears, and front-axle drive engages automatically once the rear wheels begin to slip by more than 4 per cent. Note springing for each front wheel.

Volgograd The DT 75M is the largest crawler from Volgograd and has a 7·45 litre four-cylinder 101·5 SAE hp diesel. It has seven forward and one reverse gears giving up to 11·2 km/h. A three-point linkage and PTO are fitted, and starting is by a 0·6 hp donkey engine.

Volvo BM T500 has a four-cylinder 67 SAE hp (61 DIN hp) diesel, planetary final drive, and eight forward and four reverse speed transmission. Optional Trac Trol transmission gives double that number of shift-on-the-move gears. The cab and all its contents and hydrostatic controls are built as an entirely separate unit, which is then connected to the frame of the tractor via rubber isolators.

White 4-180 Field Boss has Caterpillar V-8 diesel engine of 210 SAE hp (180 PTO hp), and two-range transmission giving twelve forward and four reverse gears, and a top speed of 18·9 mph. It has a 6000-lb implement lift and independent 1000 rpm PTO. It can pivot-steer in a 32-ft circle, and low centre of gravity transmission drives in line direct to each axle and requires only two universal joints and no transfer boxes.

Volvo BM The T700 has a 4·2 litre four-cylinder turbocharged diesel developing 96 SAE hp (90 DIN hp) and similar transmission options to the T500. The cab has a heater and defroster. The hydraulic linkage provides 6050-lb lift.

White, USA
Grey and silver

White is a comparatively recent name to tractors though some of the firms that it has acquired date from the earliest years, and indeed one of the founders of the truck side of the firm designed the Cleveland motor-cultivator over sixty years ago.

White's direct interest in tractors started in 1960, when it purchased the Oliver Corporation, whose tractor-making history dates from 1929. In that year Oliver had merged with a number of other implement-makers and, with Hart-Parr, who are credited with one of the first successful production tractors in 1902. This was made on the site of today's White tractor factory at Charles City, Iowa. In 1963 White bought the makers of Minneapolis-Moline tractors, a firm which itself had grown from a 1929 merger of tractor and implement-makers.

Since 1966 the White name has appeared on new models, as well as many Oliver and Minneapolis-Moline tractors, and is gradually replacing these names. White now concentrates on the medium and heavy end of the tractor market, catering for the lighter end in USA/Canada with tractors built for them by Fiat.

White makes various two-wheel drive models from 70 to 155 PTO hp. Shown is the 2-105 which has a 354 co. in. turbocharged six-cylinder diesel developing 105 PTO hp. Standard six-speed transmission gives eighteen forward gears with three-range hydraulic-shift; two speed PTO is fitted. Example shown has four-wheel drive.

Zetor, Czechoslovakia
Red with beige cab and mechanical parts

The first Zetor tractor, the model Twenty Five, was introduced in 1946. Now Zetors are in use in seventy countries and are one of the best-known tractors from a communist country in the West. They make 50- to 120-bhp two- and four-wheel drive models. Certain models are sold in the USA as Long, with blue livery.

ZT, East Germany
Red and pale grey

In the mid-sixties, previous tractor-manufacturing facilities in the German Democratic Republic were discontinued and production concentrated on the new ZT 300 and its derivatives. These, and East German agricultural equipment in general, are marketed under the name Fortschritt.

Zetor The 5718 has a four-cylinder 3120 cc 50-bhp diesel engine and is also available as the 5748 with four-wheel drive. It has ten forward and two reverse gears, and two-speed PTO.

ZT 303 is the 4 × 4 version of the 300 and both have four-cylinder 6560 cc 90 DIN hp diesels made under West German MAN licence by VEB IFA at Nordhausen. A three-range gearbox gives nine forward and six reverse ratios; 540/1000 rpm PTO is standard. Front-wheel drive is automatically engaged when the rear wheels begin to slip.

Zetor The 8045 Crystal 4 × 4 and its two-wheel drive sister, the 8011, share four-cylinder 4562 cc diesel engines developing 85 bhp. They have eight forward and four reverse gears, and a torque multiplier giving an additional reduction of 1 : 1·34 in every gear. 540/1000 rpm PTO is standard.

Fifty years and radically different power-farming techniques separate these two photographs. The early twenties' **International** Junior towing two-seed drills had a four-cylinder engine developing up to 30 bhp. The current **MRS** has six cylinders, all-wheel-drive and all-wheel-steer, and develops no less than 322 bhp.

ADDRESSES

AUSTRALIA

Chamberlain John Deere Pty Ltd
Welshpool Road, Welshpool, Western
Australia 6106

AUSTRIA

Reformwerke Bauer & Co GmbH
Postfach 192, Haidestrasse 40, A-4600
Wels, Durchwal

Steyr-Daimler-Puch AG
Verkauf Traktoren und Landmaschinen,
4300 St Valentin

BRAZIL

Companhia Brasileira de Tratores (CBT)
Km 249 Da Rodovia SP 318 Caixa
Postal 376, São Carlos 13.560, São
Paulo

**Malves S/A Comércio e Ind. de
Máquinas**
Av. Ipiranga, 318–20 andar-Bloco A,
São Paulo

BULGARIA

Agromachinaimpex (Bolgar)
Aksakov Str., Sofia 5

CANADA

Massey-Ferguson Industries Ltd
Toronto, Ontario M6K 1E3

Versatile Mfg Ltd
1260 Clarence Avenue, Winnipeg,
Manitoba R3T 1T3

CHINA

**China National Machinery Import and
Export Corp (Dongfeng)**
14 Chang Teh Tao, Ho Ping District,
Tientsin

CZECHOSLOVAKIA

**Liberecké Automobilové Závody
(LIAZ)**
Jablonec nad Nisou

ZKL (Zetor)
Brno (sold to the West by Motokov,
Prague)

EAST GERMANY

VEB Tractorenwerk (ZT)
33 Schönebeck/Elbe

FINLAND

Valmet Oy
Jyväskylä, PO Box 60

FRANCE

Ets. G. Ballu
49 Rue Chaude-Ruelle, 51 Epernay

Bobard Jeune SA
17 Rue de Réon, 21204 Beaune

W. et J-M Dehondt
Crasville-la-Mallet, 76450 Cany

Gévarm & St Chamond
Ste. Gevarm, 42260 St Germain Laval

Labourier et Cie
39330 Mouchard, Jura

Ets. Patissier (Energic)
51 Rue Schuman, 601 Villefranche-sur-
Saone

Regie Nationale des Usines Renault
Division Materiel Agricole, 7 Rue
Dewoitine, 78140 Velizy-Villacoublay,
RC Paris 55 B 8620

**La Société TECNOMA (Tecnoma
Derot)**
Boite Postale 195, 51321 Epernay

ITALY

Adriatica Officina Meccanica
Via Emilia al Km 16,5, 47020 Longiano
(Forli')

Agrifull SpA
Via Marconi 35, 44100 Ferrara

Bertolini Macchine Agricole SpA
Via Guicciardi 7, 42100 Reggio Emilia

Bruno Nibbi e Figli Snc
Via Fratelli Bandiera, 42110 Reggio
Emilia

Carraro SpA
Via Caltana 18, 35011 Campodarsego
(Padova)

Corghi Elettromeccanica
Casella Postale 34, Correggio, 42015
Reggio Emilia

**Fabbrica Automobili Isotta Fraschini e
Motori Breda SpA (Ranger)**
Sezione Macchine Agricole CAB, Via
Milano 7, Saronno

**Fabbrica Macchine Agricole Valpadana
SpA**
S. Martino in Rio, 42018 Reggio Emilia

Fiat Trattori SpA
Viale Torino 2, Stupinigi (To 10040)

C. Folli
Via della Repubblica 64, Casalmaggiore
(CR)

Goldoni SpA
Migliarina di Carpa, 41012 Modena

**Industrie Metallurgiche Meroni e C.
SpA (Eron)**
Sezione Trattori Eron, Via Monginevro
121, 10141 Torino

Lamborghini Trattori SpA
Via Provinciale per Bologna 9, 40066
Pieve di Cento (Bologna)

Mailam SpA
Via Marconi 29, Musile de Piave, 30024
Venezia

Massey-Ferguson-Landini SpA
Landini Division, Via C. Colombo 436,
Rome

Officine di Casaralta SpA
Sezione Trattori CAST, Via Rerrase 205,
40128 Bologna

Officine Meccaniche Ferrari
42045 Luzzara (Reggio Emilia)

PGS Motozappatrici SpA
Cadeo, 29010 Piacenza

Pinza, Benito
Via Cervese 1669, 47023 Cesena
(Forli')

SAME SpA
24047 Treviglio

Venieri, Ferdinando
Piazza Garibaldi 9, 48022 Lugo
(Ravenna)

JAPAN

**Iseki Agricultural Machinery Mfg. Co
Ltd**
1–3 Nihonbashi, 2-chome, Chuo-ku,
Tokyo, 103

Komatsu Ltd
No 3–6, 2-chome, Akasaka, Minato-ku
Tokyo

Kubota Ltd
22 Funade-cho, 2-chome, Naniwa-ku,
Osaka

Mitsubishi Motors Corp
33–8, 5-chome, Shiba, Minato-ku,
Tokyo

Satoh Agricultural Machine Mfg Co Ltd
Hibiya Kokusai Bldg No 2, 2-chome,
Uchisaiwai-cho, Chiyoda-ku, Tokyo

Toyosha Co Ltd (Hinomoto)
55 Joshoji-16, Kadoma City, Osaka 571

POLAND

**Zrzeszenie Przemystu Ciagnikowego
Ursus**
05-811 Ursus k/Warszawy, ul.,
Traktorzystow

ROMANIA

**Uzina Tracturol Brasov (UTB)
(Universal)**
Bucharest

SPAIN

Chrysler España SA (Barreiros)
Apartado 140, Villaverde, Madrid 21

Motor Iberica SA (Ebro)
Avda. Capitan Lopez Varela 149,
Barcelona 5

SWEDEN

Volvo BM AB
Eskilstuna

SWITZERLAND

Aebi & Co SA
3400 Burgdorf

Bührer Traktorenfabrik AG
8340 Hinwil, Zurich

Caterpillar Overseas SA
PO Box 408, 1211 Geneva 3

Hans Hurlimann
Lindengut, 9500 Wil

Maschinenfabrik Schilter AG
Ch-6370 Stans

UNITED KINGDOM

Aveling Marshall Ltd
Britannia Works, Gainsborough, Lincs,
DN21 2EN

Bray Construction Machinery Ltd
London Road
Tetbury, Glos, GL8 8JD

**British Leyland UK Ltd, Tractor
Operations**
Bathgate, West Lothian EH48 2EF,
Scotland

County Commercial Cars Ltd
Fleet, Hampshire

David Brown Tractors Ltd
Meltham, Huddersfield HD7 3AR, Yorks

Ford Tractor Operations
Basildon, Essex SS14 3AD

International Harvester Co
259 City Road, London EC1P 1AD

Massey-Ferguson UK
Banner Lane,
Coventry, CV4 9GF

Muir-Hill Ltd
Bristol Road, Gloucester GL1 5RX

Roadless Traction Ltd
717 London Road, Hounslow, Mddx,
TW3 1SB

J. J. Thomas & Associates
Great Bourton, Banbury, Oxon

UNITED STATES OF AMERICA

**Allis-Chalmers Agricultural Tractor
Division**
Box 512, Milwaukee, Wisconsin 53201

J. I. Case Company
700 State Street, Racine, Wisconsin
53404

Caterpillar Tractor Co
100 NE Adams St, Peoria, Illinois
61629

Deere & Company (John Deere)
Moline, Illinois

Ford Motor Co
2500 East Maple Avenue, Troy,
Michigan

Hagie Manufacturing Co
Box 273, Clarion, Iowa 50525

Hefty Tractor Co
PO Box 4189, Madison, Wisconsin
53711

International Harvester Co
South Michigan Avenue, Chicago,
Illinois

W. F. Larson Inc (Versa Tractors)
PO Box 1967, Plainview, Texas 79072

Long Manufacturing NC Inc
PO Box 1139, Tarboro, NC 27886

Minneapolis-Moline Division
White Farm Equipment Co, Charles
City, Iowa

MRS Manufacturing Co
PO Box 199, Flora, Miss. 39071

Oliver Division
White Farm Equipment Co, Charles
City, Iowa

Steiger Tractor Inc
Fargo, N.D.58102, 3101 1st Ave. No.

White Farm Equipment
White Motor Corp, Oak Brook, Illinois

USSR

Kharkov Tractor Works
Kharkov and V/o Tractoroexport,
Moscow

Kirov Tractor Works
Leningrad and V/o Tractoroexport, Moscow

Minsk Tractor Works (Belarus)
Byelorussia and V/o Tractoroexport,
Moscow

The Vladimir Tractor Works
Vladimirov, Neurostoliitto and V/o
Tractoroexport, Moscow

Volgograd Tractor Works
Volgograd and V/o Tractoroexport,
Moscow

WEST GERMANY

Agria-Werke GmbH
7108 Moeckmuehl/Wertt.

Daimler-Benz AG (Mercedes-Benz)
Stuttgart-Untertürkheim

X. Fendt & Co
8952 Marktoberdorf

**Gebr. Eicher Traktoren und
Landmaschinen-Werke GmbH**
8011 Forstern, Upper Bavaria

Gebr. Holder GmbH & Co
Postfach 66, D 7418 Metzingen

Gutbrod-Werke GmbH
6601 Saarbrücken-Bübingen, Postfach
60

Hermann Lanz Schlepperfabrik (Hela)
7960 Aulendorf, Postfach 23

Karl Blank KG
6711 Dirmstein/Pfalz

Klockner-Humboldt-Deutz AG
5000 Cologne, Postfach 80 05 09

Kramer-Werke GmbH
Postfach 1428, 7770
Überlingen/Bodensee

**Motorenfabrik Anton Schlüter
München**
Werk Freising, 8050 Freising, Postfach
2049

YUGOSLAVIA

Bratstvo
Masinsko-Metalurski Kombinat, 72280
Novi Travnik

Industrija i Traktora (IMT)
Belgrade

ABBREVIATIONS

bhp=brake horsepower
hp=horsepower
DIN, BS, AU, SAE, etc. following the bhp/hp rating indicate the official standards governing the measurement
PTO=power take off
Q-cab=sound insulated cab
TVO=tractor vapourising oil
4×4=four-wheeler with all wheels driven
4×2=four-wheeler with two driven
6×4=six-wheeler with four driven